The Many Facets of Prayer

Part One

Jill Curry

THE MANY FACETS OF PRAYER

PART ONE

Touching Heaven
from the
Secret Place

Front cover design and artwork: Denise Perentin and Jill Curry. Eagle photo by Matthew Schwartz NEvS5lHyrlk on Unsplash (Part 2 only).

Copyright © 2025 J.M. Curry. All rights reserved. Copies can be obtained through www.giftsfortheking.com.au or through Koorong Books. Jill can be contacted through the website.

This book or any portion thereof may not be reproduced or used in any manner whatsoever without the express written permission of the publisher except for the use of brief quotations in a book review.

First printing 2025

ISBN: 978-0-9945758-5-2

Bible verses quoted are taken from the NASB 2020 unless otherwise noted.

"Scripture quotations taken from the (NASB®) New American Standard Bible®, Copyright © 1960, 1971, 1977, 1995, 2020 by The Lockman Foundation. Used by permission. All rights reserved. www.lockman.org"

Bible verses marked NIV or NIV(UK):

Scripture quotations marked (NIV) are taken from the Holy Bible, New International Version®, NIV®. Copyright © 1973, 1978, 1984, 2011 by Biblica, Inc.™ Used by permission of Zondervan. All rights reserved worldwide. www.zondervan.com The "NIV" and "New International Version" are trademarks registered in the United States Patent and Trademark Office by Biblica, Inc.™

Endorsements

The Many Facets of Prayer is probably one of the most comprehensive books on prayer I have ever seen. It is definitely the greatest encyclopaedic book on prayer ever written in Australia. It is a great resource for passionate prayer warriors or those desiring to step up and stand in the gap on behalf of the land.

Warwick Marsh, is the Co-founder and Director of The Canberra Declaration www.canberradeclaration.org.au. He is also the Co-founder of the National Day of Prayer and Fasting and founder of Dads4Kids Fatherhood Foundation. In 1998 he received a Father of the Year Award in the NSW Parliament and in 2001 he was a recipient of a Centenary Medal from the Prime Minister for his mission work and his work with Aboriginal people and youth.

Jill Curry is a respected author and leader in the prayer movement in Australia and beyond. Her latest book *The Many Facets of Prayer* brings together the rich deposit of all she has learnt about prayer over many years of walking with the Lord. Stressing that our role is to prepare the way in prayer for Christ's return, she highlights the importance of learning to hear His voice, and walking intimately with Him.

Written as a daily devotional, the book offers different themes and relating scriptures upon which to meditate, with added teaching on each aspect. Prayer leaders will appreciate the author's wisdom and experience when it comes to leading prayer meetings. She encourages us that, 'There is much more to prayer that is rarely explored.'

The book is a treasure chest of wide-ranging instructions of all you need to know as you seek the Father in prayer, for the advancement of His Kingdom here on earth.

Jennifer Hagger AM is the Founder and former Director of the Australian House of Prayer for All Nations, and Mission World Aid. She is a Member of The Global Watch Advisory Council.

I have had the privilege of reading *The Many Facets of Prayer* by Jill Curry. It is a stunning and comprehensive look at prayer and prayer strategy.

For those that need a powerful prayer resource this book is for you. It starts with foundational concepts such as hearing from God, then guides you through subjects like His will, forgiveness, agreement, alignment, discipline, obedience, waiting, thankfulness, worship, confession, perseverance, et. al. Then building on those precepts teaches powerful prayer strategies for praying with and for others, workplace prayer, spiritual warfare, praying for cities and regions, prophetic prayer, and praying for nations.

The book provides an easy to comprehend, but also deep understanding of what prayer is to the intercessor prayer warrior in God's Kingdom.

Jill's work provides a military grade training manual for prophetic prayer warriors; I highly recommend this book to all Christian leaders and those with an intercessory calling. Once published I will be encouraging all our National Prayer Team to get a copy.

Kym Farnik, together with his wife, Nel, are the national prayer coordinators for Canberra Declaration. They are active in local, national, and global ministries and have ministered in various nations including Kenya, Uganda, and Israel. www.canberradeclaration.org.au

----

The Many Facets of Prayer is a teaching devotional on prayer that is easy to read, comprehensive in its scope and always leaves the reader encouraged, with a greater hunger to know God and to be effective in prayer. In my mind, each devotion is like filling one's mouth with a deep draught of the best reserve red wine and mulling it around to enjoy the full flavour and to savour the aftertaste. Each daily devotional is to be read, dwelt on and savoured, to get the full impact of the teaching and prayer.

I have known Jill for many years and have been with her in a regular weekly prayer gathering that meets on zoom. Jill prays out of the depth of her relationship with the Lord, her devotion to the Word of God and with clear prophetic insight. *The Many Facets of Prayer* contains rich gems gleaned by Jill over her years of being a devoted and faithful follower and servant of Yeshua. It will deepen and strengthen your life of prayer.

Karen Wilson, is a retired Pastor and Bible College teacher at Stairway Church, Melbourne and remains involved in her home church in prayer and prayer ministry. She is also a leader and occasional teacher on The Global Watch.

Prayer is one of the most powerful tools a human can have. It is allowing us to connect with the Creator of the universe to find our true destiny. This book is a great read for anyone wanting to understand more about the principles and power of prayer.

Ken Duncan, OAM is an internationally acclaimed photographer, who aims to capture and present the spirit and beauty of God's creation in his artworks. Ken also established the Walk a While Foundation, working with Indigenous communities in Central Australia, and assisted them in raising the forgiveness cross on Memory Mountain, near Haasts Bluff, NT. www.walkawhile.org.au

----

Jill Curry's latest book is a must have on your bedside table or on your study desk or prayer room because she has produced a masterpiece guide to prayer. A long term-prayer warrior herself, prayer leader and leader of prayer tours through Israel and other nations, she is an expert guide. Added to that, she hears from the Lord, has a strong prophetic gift and she has no doubt prayed long over this wonderful offering. It's a perfect gift for those you love or to use in prayer groups to read an excerpt and discuss before you launch into prayer.

Barbara Miller is a pastor, prophet, mediator, psychologist, sociologist, teacher and writer. Together with her aboriginal husband, apostle and artist Norman, they founded the Centre for International Reconciliation and Peace Inc. based in Cairns and co-founded the Indigenous Friends of Israel International. www.indigenousfriendsofisrael.org

----

The new wineskin is the house of prayer! Sadly, we have made church about almost everything but prayer. Jesus said Father's house is to be a house of prayer for all nations. Prayer is meant to be the main thing!

We are in a critical time in history. For the ecclesia to arise, rather than hide, we must understand and embrace *The Many Facets of Prayer*. I pray Jill's book is a catalyst to smash every obstructive stereotype of prayer. May a new generation, of every age, gender and race, be ignited to passionately grasp the numerous ways of participating in prayer.

Ruth Webb, Tabernacle of David, Bendigo. www.tabernacleofdavid.org.au

----

This powerful and Spirit-led book is a timely gift to the Body of Christ. Rooted in Scripture and Kingdom purpose, it unveils the depth and beauty of prayer as a grace gift from God.

Jill skilfully guides readers into a lifestyle of communion with the Father, through the Holy Spirit, aligning hearts with the will of God. Her strategic insights are grounded in the Word and birthed from years of experience in prayer and intercession.

More than a manual, this is a spiritual journey, awakening readers to pray from heaven's perspective. It is like discovering light through the many facets of a diamond, that deepens their relationship with Jesus, to partner with Him for His Kingdom purposes on earth.

Dr Hilary Moroney, Director and Co-Founder, Canberra House of Prayer for all Nations, Australia.

Worthy is the Lamb,
who was slain,
to receive power and wealth
and wisdom and strength
and honour and glory and praise!

Revelation 5:12

Table of Contents

Part 1

Introduction

Section 1

Individual Prayer

1. **The uniqueness of Christian prayer** Uniqueness; Prayer from the heart; The role of the Spirit; God's character; God is holy; God is good; Golden bowls

2. **Hearing God's voice** Hearing from God; Friends with God; Walking with God; Recognising His voice; The still small voice; Dwelling with God; The bride of Christ

3. **Prerequisites of answered prayer** Ask; In His name; Faith not doubt; According to His will; Fruitful obedience; Forgiveness; Agreement

4. **Agreement with God** The only way; The nature of sin; Self-justification; Self-pity; Health; Money; Sexuality

5. **Alignment with God** In Christ; On God's side; Understanding God's plans; The way of the cross; Advancing the Kingdom; Finding our place; Watching and waiting

6. **The discipline of prayer** An imperishable prize; Crucifying the flesh; Adding character; Broken walls; Pray without ceasing; Pray in the Spirit; Be alert

7. **Obedience in prayer** Choices; Blessings of obedience; Curses of disobedience; The cost of obedience; The cost of disobedience; Generational curses; God's order

8. **Repentance and prayer** Repent; John the Baptist; Psalm 51; Sowing and reaping; Breaking curses; Prepare the way; But they refused to repent

9. **Fasting and prayer** When you fast; Why fast; Types of fasts; How to fast; The power of fasting; For such a time as this; The chosen fast

10. **Thankfulness and prayer** Enter His courts; In everything give thanks; God is faithful; The sacrifice of thanksgiving; First fruits; Finding the good in the bad; The privilege of thanksgiving

11. **Praise and prayer** Hallelujah; Telling others; Bless; Praise God inhabits; Singing and music; Shout; Physical praise

12. **Worship and prayer** Praise or worship; The secret place; Bowing down; In Spirit and truth; Reverence; Bond-servant; Heavenly worship

13. **The prayers of Jesus** Jesus' life of prayer; Praying for children; Our Father; Give us this day; High Priestly prayer; Gethsemane; Prayers from the cross

14. **Praying the Psalms** Sweet psalmist; A man after God's own heart; Psalms of praise and thanksgiving; Special occasions; A psalm for all seasons; Prophetic psalms; David's legacy

15. **Praying in tongues** Promise of the Spirit; The day of Pentecost; Gifts of the Spirit; The gift of tongues; Order in the church; Paul and tongues; The greatest gift is love

16. **Little foxes** Respectable sins; Worldliness; Apathy; Comfort; Pride; Fear of man; Taming the tongue

17. **Confession** Recognising our nature; Acknowledging specific sins; Restitution; Admitting sin to another; Confessing our faith; Confession in heaven; Every tongue will confess

18. **Perseverance** The persistent widow; Running the race; The test of endurance; The ANZACs; Finding joy; Finishing well; Joining the saints

Section 2

Praying with and for others

19. **Prayer meetings** Individual and group prayer; The flow of the Holy Spirit; Prayer partners and mentors; Small groups; Public prayer; The abuse of prayer; Leading prayer meetings

20. **Pastoral prayer** More Lord; Love one another; Prayer for the sick; Male and female; Lure of the world; Bring in the harvest; The persecuted church

21. **Prayer shield** Prayer cover; Praying for pastors; Praying for leaders; Intercessors and pastors; Those in dangerous jobs; Special assignments; Missionaries

22. **Intercession** What is intercession; Jesus our intercessor; Abraham; Moses; David; Being the answer; The ministry of reconciliation

23. **The priestly role of prayer** A Kingdom of priests; Authority to bless; Servants; The golden altar; Fire on the altar; Raise the standard; The Zadok priesthood

24. **Prayers of blessing** The power of blessing; The gift of encouragement; The Sabbath blessing; Encouraging the body; Prayers of blessing; The language of love; Building one another up

25. **Evangelism and prayer** In season and out of season; If I am lifted up; Work of the Spirit; Word and deed; Athens; Corinth; Revive us

26. **Angels and prayer** Good and bad angels; Worshipping angels; Warrior angels; Guardian angels; Messenger angels; Ministering angels; Worship the Lord

27. **Praying like Paul** Prayers of thanksgiving; Prayers of praise; Ephesians 1; Ephesians 3; Colossians, Philippians; Thessalonians; Paul's prayers for himself

28. **Travailing prayer** The price of revival; Wrestling with God; The way of no return; Birthing the promise; Believing for the supernatural; Agony; Breaking of the waters

Appendix: Prayer to commit your life to Jesus; Prayer to be filled with the Holy Spirit

Table of Contents - Part 2

Endnotes

Bibliography

Acknowledgements

About the Author

Books by the same author

Introduction

Welcome to *The Many Facets of Prayer* teaching devotional. Congratulations on having a desire to explore prayer for a whole year. That is quite a commitment and I trust the journey will be extremely fulfilling and take you to new heights in your relationship with the Lord and with other like-minded intercessors.

The book falls into two parts. The first focuses on developing an effective personal prayer life grounded in the Scriptures and discovering different facets of prayer and new ways to pray and worship the Lord. We then progress to praying for family and friends and your church, individually and in groups. The second part explores prayer in the workplace and spiritual warfare before venturing into prophetic aspects of prayer and praying for our cities, regions and nations. It is hoped each reader will complete the whole course, not just one part, as it will equip not only you for wider prayer, but train the body of Christ to reach out beyond the walls of the church to touch the world with the gospel of the Kingdom of God and take up our responsibility for our nation.

The major focus is on teaching rather than providing pre-written prayers. The aim is for you to learn to construct your own prayers, although a very short prayer or exercise is given for each day. Each week we look at a different theme. The teaching is progressive so it is highly recommended that you work through from the beginning to the end in order rather than choosing ad hoc topics. It is strongly recommended to keep a prayer diary as a record of your journey.

There are so many aspects to this wonderful gift of communication with a God who is personal, living and yearning for us to come into His presence. He always wants to show us more of who He is and reveal His ways and His plans to us, not only for our own lives, but also for our cities and nations. There are many indications that we are living in the end days about which the prophets wrote, but which they could barely conceive. God has a plan and He wants us to partner with Him to bring it to pass on the earth. The times are dark and the people need the light of God. It all starts in the prayer room as we meet with the Creator of the universe.

I trust you will discover many keys to unlock new dimensions of prayer and find that prayer is so much more exciting and wide-ranging than you ever knew before.

Enjoy the journey!

Shalom,

JILL CURRY

Section 1

Individual Prayer

Week 1
The uniqueness of Christian prayer

Week 1, Day 1: Uniqueness

Come close to God and He will come close to you. James 4:8

As we commence our journey through prayer this year, we would be wise to stop and consider how privileged we are that God would desire to be known by us and speak to us personally. This is unique among the religions of humanity, as other gods are distant, perhaps seen as a creator but not known as a personal God who desires our presence and wants us to come into a loving relationship with Him. No other religion has a God who speaks in love to His people. He does not need us but He wants us. Love needs a recipient and He longs for His love to be reciprocated.

Prayer is communication with God, not just talking to Him. We can only do this through Jesus in the power of the Holy Spirit. We can speak to a man-made idol but it will not answer us. Religious teachers throughout the ages have written volumes of books of instructions, wise sayings and their ponderings on life but all are now dead. Only Jesus was resurrected as proof that He is more than a teacher, rabbi or prophet. He is the LORD. He alone is the Way, the Truth and the Life (Jn 14:6). If you do not know God and Jesus like this, pray the prayer in the appendix.[1]

Heavenly Father, draw me close to You this day. I want to know You personally and communicate with You. I open my heart to You and ask that You speak to me this day. I thank You that Jesus died for me to restore this relationship with You.

Week 1, Day 2: Prayer from the heart

And when you are praying, do not use thoughtless repetition as the Gentiles do, for they think that they will be heard because of their many words. Matthew 6:7

Abba (meaning Daddy or Father) is not interested in religion. Jesus' greatest opponents were the religious leaders of His day. They prayed, they fasted and they tithed, but their hearts were not humble before God and they lacked the ability to communicate with Him to receive His heart for themselves and the people they served. Let us throw off the cloak of religiosity and come to the Father within the veil that was torn on the day of the crucifixion, allowing us access to the throne room of God.

Other religions chant mantras or seek to empty the mind. Beware of opening your mind to nothingness. If you like to meditate, then meditate on the Word of God and the character of God. Guard your heart so false spirits do not come in to fill a void (Matt 12:43-45).

Jesus appreciated the mite that the poor widow gave rather than the grand gifts of the wealthy (Mk 12:42). He does not want thoughtless repetitive prayers that someone else wrote. He wants our hearts. Talk to God as you would a loving parent or friend. Thank Him for His love, His creation, your friends and family and share what is on your heart today. Ask Him to share what is on His heart.

Abba Father, thank You for this new day and all it holds. Thank You for my health to enjoy it and for your love that encompasses me. May your Holy Spirit lead and guide me today. Show me what is on your heart now.

Week 1, Day 3: The role of the Holy Spirit

In the same way the Spirit also helps our weakness; for we do not know how to pray as we should, but the Spirit Himself intercedes for us with groanings too deep for words; and He who searches the hearts knows what the mind of the Spirit is, because He intercedes for the saints according to the will of God. Romans 8:26-27

We are not alone in our quest to know God more and to learn to pray effectively. It is the role of the Holy Spirit to assist us in our prayer life, so welcome Him in! This is our spirit connecting to God's Spirit. In Psalm 42:7, the psalmist, in the midst of yearning and despair, speaks of 'deep calling unto deep.'[2]

Prayer is not meant to be telling God what is on our agenda. It is an opportunity to come into His presence and bring our petitions to Him so He can provide the solutions and direct our hearts to pray aright. The Holy Spirit intercedes within us, so tune in to what He is saying. Jesus is our intercessor at God's right hand, constantly interceding for us before the Father.

It is Christ who died, and furthermore is also risen, who is even at the right hand of God, who also makes intercession for us. Rom 8:34

We need to join the prayer meeting of heaven, not ask heaven to join ours. One of the major traps that we fall into is coming to prayer with our minds made up as to how or what we should pray. We need to be in a position of an open heart so that God can direct us and have a willing heart that will obey whatever we need to do in response.

Dear Lord, let me join the intercession of heaven today. Take me to where You are and let me see and hear what is happening around your throne.

Week 1, Day 4: God's character - who we pray to

For God so loved the world, that He gave His only Son, so that everyone who believes in Him will not perish, but have eternal life. John 3:16

I remember our first tour guide in Israel. I was shivering on a winter's day and he took off his coat to loan it to me to get warm! On another occasion, I was having lunch in a café with a couple of other staff members when a former student turned up. When we went to pay, we were told all had been paid already! These small acts of unexpected kindness and generosity warmed my heart. But these are nothing in comparison to what Jesus has done for us. I stood guilty before the courts of heaven and He laid down His life in an agonising death to pay for my guilt and win a pardon for me. And that even before I knew Him (Rom 5:8). What a gracious gift!

Before we are willing to open ourselves up to someone, we need to be assured that the person is trustworthy and loving. Knowing God's character is essential to a close relationship.

Greater love has no one than this, that a person will lay down his life for his friends. Jn 15:13

Meditate on God's love today. Take communion (you are a priest – 1 Pet 2:9) and thank Him for His great love from which nothing we have done or ever will do can separate us. Rom 8:38-39

Week 1, Day 5: God is Holy

*And the four living creatures, each one of them having six wings, are full of eyes around and within; and day and night they do not cease to say, 'Holy, holy, holy is the L*ORD *God, the Almighty, who was and who is and who is to come.'* Revelation 4:8

The most common character trait of God praised by the heavenly beings is His holiness. It is also the quintessential characteristic of the Holy Spirit.

The primary meaning of *qodesh* (holiness) is to set apart for sacred service. Holy vessels, garments or people must be untainted by imperfections and could not be used for any other purpose. God is separate and apart from all His creation because He is sinless and sin cannot enter His presence. Someone who sets themselves apart for Him must disentangle themselves from evil and sin. Of ourselves, this is impossible, but God imparted His own righteousness to us at our salvation when we believed in Jesus (Phil 3:9) so we can now have fellowship with the Father. Living a holy life means hating sin, but will assure us of living life to its fullest.

There is a frequent biblical connection between holiness and fear. This is a healthy, reverential awe that recognises that God is a righteous judge who must punish sin as it separates us from Him. God is a consuming fire! To lose this fear is to accept cheap grace. The book of Romans expands this concept.

Father, let me stand in awe of You today. You are majestic, holy, awesome and perfect love. Thank You, Jesus for imparting your righteousness to me. May I not treat this lightly.

Week 1, Day 6: God is Good

..."*He indeed is good for His lovingkindness is everlasting,*" *then the house...of the Lord was filled with a cloud, so that the priests could not stand to minister...for the glory of the Lord filled the house of God.* 2 Chronicles 5:13-14

When Moses came down the mountain with the two tablets, he was angry with the people who had made and worshiped the golden calf image in his absence and he did not want to go on. He interceded for the people and he was assured of angels to accompany them, but he sought to see God face to face and implored God to show him His glory.

Then Moses said, 'Please, show me Your glory!' And He said, "I Myself will make all My goodness pass before you, and will proclaim the name of the LORD *before you; and I will be gracious to whom I will be gracious, and will show compassion to whom I will show compassion."* Ex 33:18-19

God granted his wish and showed him His goodness and loving kindness. God is always good and can only be good. He is not changeable. Sometimes when things fall apart, we want to blame God. Our own shortcomings or sometimes satanic interference are the most likely causes that mess up God's good plans. God is the one who fixes our messes, not causes them. In our prayers, we need to be assured of His good character in order to pray correctly. He always works to bring the best for us.

Look at Psalm 136. Try writing your own version with your own life story and thanking God for His goodness and lovingkindness.

Week 1, Day 7: Golden bowls

When He had taken the scroll, the four living creatures and the twenty-four elders fell down before the Lamb, each one holding a harp and golden bowls full of incense, which are the prayers of the saints. Revelation 5:8

The Old Testament tabernacle and later the temple were patterns of the heavenly temple. Each of the objects in it show us how we should approach God. In Exodus chapter 30 there was a golden altar which was to burn the incense. This was a fragrant aroma placed before the veil separating the room where the ark or throne of God resided.

If we wonder what happens to our prayers, the book of Revelation assures us that our prayers are the incense in heaven, gathered into the golden bowls and presented before God's throne. Our prayers are not discarded, and even if we forget what we pray for, God does not. It is the prayers of the saints that lead to the sounding of the seven trumpets which precede the return of Christ to earth as the King of kings to begin His royal reign (Rev 8:3). Our role is to prepare the way in prayer for His coming and the bringing of the Kingdom rule, which is now in heaven, to earth as Jesus directed us in the Lord's prayer (Matt 6:10). Our prayers matter. The practice of prayer is joining heaven and earth and preparing us to be conduits of His Kingdom here. Our lives are His fragrance to the world around us.

For we are a fragrance of Christ to God among those who are being saved... 2 Cor 2:15a

Dear Lord Jesus, help me not take my responsibility lightly but to realise the centrality of prayer and the importance of a prayerful life. Make me a conduit for your Kingdom today.

The Many Facets of Prayer

Week 2
Hearing God's voice

Week 2, Day 1: Hearing from God

My sheep hear My voice, and I know them, and they follow Me. John 10:27

Our journey of prayer is grounded in hearing from God, not just talking to Him. Though absolutely crucial to our walk with God, most of us struggle with hearing from heaven. Whether it is busyness, apathy, ignorance, lack of self-discipline or the spirit of religion that gets in the way, we find it much easier to attend a prayer meeting, go through a ritual quiet time or just talk *to* God rather than hear *from* Him. Perhaps we believe that God only speaks to us today through the Bible and guides us through circumstances. Because we lack this personal relationship, we may run to find the latest article from recognised preachers, teachers, prophets or TV evangelists, but we do not see ourselves as worthy of God wanting to speak to us personally.

The good news is that He does care and He wants to share His love with us personally and not be a distant, mystic entity that created the world and will meet us at the end of life. If we seek intimacy with Him and desire to enter His presence, He will be faithful and meet us under the wings of the cherubim. The curtain was torn in the temple when Jesus died on the cross and we do not need to be a high priest now to come into the throne room of the Father. He will extend the golden sceptre to us if we enter through the blood of the Lamb who was slain to pay the price for our sin.

Thank You, Jesus, for restoring the way to meet with Abba Father. I repent of false beliefs that have caused me to keep God at a distance. I want a deep, personal relationship with You and I open my heart to receive your love today. I love You. Wait, listen then journal what He says.

Week 2, Day 2: Friends with God

No longer do I call you slaves, for the slave does not know what his master is doing; but I have called you friends, because all things that I have heard from My Father I have made known to you. John 15:15

What a privilege this is! Jesus wants to enfold us into His circle of friends and continue to pass on to us all that He hears from the Father. His desire is not just to give us commands to follow but to entrust us with the things that are on His heart and hear from us the things that concern us!

Friends share their hearts and make time to listen to one another. They are there in times of trouble and share in our joy and celebrations. They share our burdens and accept us as we are with all our blemishes and shortcomings.

The LORD used to speak to Moses face to face, just as a man speaks to his friend. Ex 33:11

We don't have to be a Moses, called to deliver a nation from slavery, but we can now see God face to face, if we are willing to walk with Jesus.

Dear Jesus, I know that I am not worthy to be called your friend but I thank You for this great privilege. Cleanse my heart of all that displeases You and help me to live in purity with You. Teach me your ways that I may walk with You. Show me how I can be more like You. Open my ears to hear from You, to know You more and to trust You more deeply.

Week 2, Day 3: Walking with God

Now they heard the sound of the LORD *God walking in the garden in the cool of the day, and the man and his wife hid themselves from the presence of the* LORD *God among the trees of the garden.* Genesis 3:8

God has a garden of Eden for us where we can meet with Him and talk with Him. Satan is not afraid of 'religion' but will do all He can to deceive us with 'did God say?' (Gen 3:1). He will throw every distraction our way to stop us from coming into the presence of the Lord. It is good to set aside a specific place and time and stick to it, preferably in the morning. You may like to put an extra chair in the room in expectation of Jesus coming to sit with you.

I am God Almighty; walk before Me, and be blameless. I will make My covenant between Me and you, and I will multiply you exceedingly. Gen 17:1-2

When God called Abraham to walk with Him, it was into a covenant relationship. He had to walk by faith and believe for the supernatural. Our walk will also involve the same, if we do not shirk from what God may call us to do.

Walking with Him also involves turning away from sin of every kind. Adam and Eve could not face a holy God after their disobedience. Many are afraid to come into God's presence because they fear He will be angry. We cannot hide from God but sin separates us from Him. Be quick to repent and ask God to fill the desire to sin with His presence so you do not resort to what grieves Him. He will gently speak to you. He sees your heart, forgives, and as with the repentant King David, He will welcome those with a contrite heart into His presence.

Lord Jesus, show me where I need to change to be more like You. Ps 51

Week 2, Day 4: Recognising His voice

But the Helper, the Holy Spirit, whom the Father will send in My name, He will teach you all things, and bring to your remembrance all that I said to you. John 14:26

One of the greatest dilemmas for many Christians is knowing whether what they hear is the voice of God, their own voice or that of Satan trying to lead them astray. Like any relationship, it takes time, trial and error and determined effort on our part to want to know God. As we practise, we become better at recognising the voice of our Friend, and less likely to be deceived by anyone else trying to impersonate Him. The more we know the character and track record of God, the less likely we are to be deceived or side-tracked by Satan or his assistants.

God never goes against His Word, so the more the Bible becomes part of us, the better the chance we have of hearing correctly. A text may jump out as we read, the Holy Spirit may bring a verse to memory, or God may lead us to a book, chapter, event or concept to study through the Scriptures. God can speak to us through the body of Christ, dreams or visions, or at odd times through an audible voice, angels, nature or circumstances, but mostly it is just a thought or impression, prompted by the Holy Spirit. Those who hear God's voice clearly are not extra-ordinary people but ordinary people who trust an extraordinary God.

Lord God, I am listening. I ask You to speak to me. Write down and follow what He prompts in your spirit.

Week 2, Day 5: The still small voice

And after the earthquake a fire, but the LORD was not in the fire; and after the fire a still small voice. 1 Kings 19:12 (NKJV)

As in the days of Elijah, God does not often speak in a voice like an earthquake or appear in a ball of fire, but He more often speaks as a gentle breeze. Wind, breath and spirit, *ruach* in Hebrew, are all the same word. That means that to hear the voice of God, we need to listen very carefully. We cannot see the wind, only its effects, but we do hear it.

We also need to clear our mind of pre-conceived ideas or biases that can block our hearing. We cannot dictate to God what He should tell us, though we can ask Him questions. He is always more interested in winning our hearts than engaging in intellectual discussions. We also need to be aware that the Hebrew way of answering a question is with another question. Jesus used this style of teaching many times amongst His disciples and also with the Scribes and Pharisees. So be prepared for some probing questions!

Look for where the wind of the Spirit is blowing today. God is always at work in His world. When you see that, ask Him how He would have you respond. Does a neighbour have a need where you can help? Is someone at work in need of a hug or a listening ear? It is these little things that God uses to train us in listening and obeying His voice.

Heavenly Father, quiet my rambling thoughts and train me to hear and obey your voice.

Week 2, Day 6: Dwelling with God

... that He would grant you, according to the riches of His glory, to be strengthened with power through His Spirit in the inner self, so that Christ may dwell in your hearts through faith; and that you, being rooted and grounded in love, may...know the love of Christ... Ephesians 3:16- 17, 19a

It was always God's desire to share His paradise with His human creation. He commanded Moses to build a tabernacle so that He could meet with the people.

I will dwell among...Israel and will be their God. Then they shall know that I am the Lord their God who brought them out of...Egypt, that I might dwell among them. Ex 29:45-46

Our bodies are now the temple of the Holy Spirit (1 Cor 6:19) so we need to keep the temple holy. Are there any rooms in your temple where Jesus would not be comfortable? If so, clean up now. Is there any talk in your household that does not honour God? Guard your lips. Are there hidden thoughts or actions that do not reflect the light of God? Then it is time for change.

Many decades ago, there was a book and arm bands that said, 'What would Jesus do?' If we keep this question in our minds each day as we go about our daily tasks, it will assist our decision making and our walk with God. In all things, we should seek to glorify God. If faced with a dilemma, take the path that would give God the most glory and you will not go wrong.

Anna was one who wanted to dwell in the courts of the Lord and she recognised the Redeemer of Israel and declared Him to all (Lk 2:36-38). By dwelling in His presence, we will also gain spiritual perception.

Abba Father, I seek your face and your presence this day. Come Lord Jesus. Ps 27:4ff

Week 2, Day 7: The bride of Christ

He has brought me to his banquet hall, and his banner over me is love. Song of Solomon 2:4

One doesn't become a bride through a casual relationship with someone. That person will become our helpmeet and intimate partner for the rest of our lives – or that is how it is supposed to be! The Lord is returning for a bride. When we see ourselves in that light, it will change how we approach the Lord and transform our prayer life.

In preparing for a wedding, there is much to organise and decide, but we do not do that alone. The preparation time is one of learning what the partner likes, sharing our thoughts and desires, knitting our hearts together and learning to work as one. We grow in love as we do so.

This time on earth is a preparation for the great marriage supper of the Lamb that awaits us. In an ancient Jewish wedding, the bridegroom sends gifts to the bride-to-be so she can adorn herself for the wedding. We will reflect His image and be carriers of His glory. What gifts has the Lord given you? Are you using them to bring Him glory?

Let's rejoice and be glad and give the glory to Him, because the marriage of the Lamb has come, and His bride has prepared herself. Rev 19:7

Dear Lord, please show me how to prepare my heart to be a beautiful bride for You, my heavenly Bridegroom. I give all that I am to You. Fill me with your love and help me to love You as You love me.

Week 3

Prerequisites of answered prayer

Week 3, Day 1: Ask

So do not be like them [the Pharisees]; for your Father knows what you need before you ask Him. Matthew 6:8

If God knows our needs, why should we pray at all? He desires above all that we have relationship with Him and communication is at the centre of that relationship. He could do all things without us but He wants us to be willing partners with Him in bringing the Kingdom of heaven to earth through us. How exciting!

God loves to answer our prayers. He wants us to know that He is good and to pour out His love on us. This gives us confidence to come before Him in prayer.

What man is there among you who, when his son asks for a loaf, will give him a stone? Or if he asks for a fish, he will not give him a snake, will he? If you then, being evil, know how to give good gifts to your children, how much more will your Father who is in heaven give what is good to those who ask Him! Matt 7:9-11

In order to have our prayers answered, there are certain biblical prerequisites. The first is simply to ask! This should be obvious, but how often do we complain, but not actually pray?

Ask, and it will be given to you; seek, and you will find; knock, and it will be opened to you. For everyone who asks receives, and he who seeks finds, and to him who knocks it will be opened. Matt 7:7-8

Dear Father, please forgive me for grumbling instead of talking to You. Make me into a house of prayer. Mk 11:17

Week 3, Day 2: In His name

Whatever you ask in My name, that will I do, so that the Father may be glorified in the Son. If you ask Me anything in My name, I will do it. John 14:13-14

Asking in Jesus' name is not a magic spell or a formula that we attach as a postscript at the end of our prayers. His name has to do with His authority. Jesus observed what the Father was doing and then He did likewise (Jn 5:19). Effective prayer originates in heaven. As an ambassador represents the country that sends him abroad, so our prayers need to be commissioned from the throne room. We approach the Father through Jesus, who is interceding for us at the right hand of the Father (Rom 8:34). Because He shed His blood for us, He is worthy to intercede for us before the Father's throne.

The other qualification in this passage is that our prayers need to give glory to God. Then it will be His joy to grant us our requests. If we are abiding in Him as the branches are attached to the vine, we will be fed by the sap and lifeblood of Jesus flowing through us.

If you abide in Me, and My words abide in you, ask whatever you wish, and it will be done for you. Jn 15:7 (NASB 1995)

Dear Lord Jesus, thank You for interceding for me before the throne of God. Open my ears to hear the prayers You are praying, that I may join You in your intercession. Matt 6:7-15

Week 3, Day 3: Faith, not doubt

Jesus answered saying to them, 'Have faith in God...whoever says to this mountain, "Be...cast into the sea," and does not doubt..., but believes that what he says is going to happen, it will be granted him. Therefore, I say to you, all things for which you pray and ask, believe that you have received them, and they will be granted you.' Mark 11:22-24 See also Matthew 21:21-22 (NASB 1995)

The antidote to doubt is to ask for a deeper revelation of the Father's heart. Faith comes when we know the faithfulness and character of God. If we doubt His character, we will doubt that He will answer. Our faith must be faith in God, not in our own faith or our own goodness to deserve anything. Faith is not just hope, but an assurance that God has heard us and will answer (Heb 11:1). We rarely doubt that God *can* grant what we ask, but rather that He *will* answer us.

Sometimes we lack certainty that it is really God speaking and not just our own will. When God calls us, it will always be too big for us! Otherwise, we would not require faith and not rely on Him. If the request will glorify Jesus, we are on safe ground. It may take time to come to the place of assurance, but when we know God has spoken and truly believe that He wants to answer our prayers, then we can already begin to praise Him for the upcoming answer.

The epileptic boy's father cried, 'I do believe; help my unbelief.' (Mk 9:20-25). So I too, Lord, ask You to help me to grow in faith and believe for the 'greater works.' Jn 14:12

Week 3, Day 4: According to His will

This is the confidence which we have before Him, that, if we ask anything according to His will, He hears us. And if we know that He hears us in whatever we ask, we know that we have the requests which we have asked from Him. 1 John 5:14-15

Knowing the will of God again comes back to knowing the character and the Word of God. When the written Word and the living Word are embedded in our hearts, we will recognise the voice of the Shepherd, and know how He operates, which is rarely according to the ways of the world. We need to seek to know God's will in every matter and pray accordingly. 'If it be your will' is mostly a cop out prayer for *not* knowing His will! Jesus only prayed 'if it be your will' when He knew exactly what He had to do! He was asking that if there were any other way to achieve the Father's purpose and spare Him the agony of the cross, then let that come to pass, but if not – then let your will be done. We must also be willing to go the way of the cross in order to see God's glorious victory and miraculous answers.

You do not have because you do not ask. You ask and do not receive, because you ask with wrong motives, so that you may spend it on your pleasures. Jas 4:2b-3

If our motives in prayer are for our own selfish gain (not just needs) and not that God may be glorified and His Kingdom extended, we need to stop and do a heart check.

Purify my heart, Lord, and make me willing to suffer if necessary for your will to be done on earth as it is in heaven. Help me truly to seek first the Kingdom of God. Matt 6:31-33

Week 3, Day 5: Fruitful obedience

You did not choose Me but I chose you, and appointed you that you would go and bear fruit, and that your fruit would remain, so that whatever you ask of the Father in My name He may give to you. John 15:16

Bearing fruit for His Kingdom comes from abiding in the vine, remaining attached to the stem and the root, and not becoming independent and proud. If we are faithful in the small things, the Lord can entrust us with more, which will mean more productivity.

Beloved, if our heart does not condemn us, we have confidence before God; and whatever we ask we receive from Him, because we keep His commandments and do the things that are pleasing in His sight. 1 Jn 3:21-22

If we are not getting answers to our prayers, it is worthwhile checking if we have obeyed what He has previously asked us to do. Why should He give us more instructions if we have not done the last thing He asked? God wants us to become the answer to our prayer. He is more interested in our hearts than just ticking the boxes of answered prayers. We tend to be more concerned about God intervening to change others who are difficult, or alter circumstances that are problematic than allowing Him to do a deep work of circumcision of our own hearts. Perhaps we need to overcome a fear, change a heart attitude or reconcile a broken relationship before He can answer.

Father, I give You permission to take the scalpel and cut out anything that is not pleasing to You. Matt 5:22-24

Week 3, Day 6: Forgiveness

Whenever you stand praying, forgive, if you have anything against anyone, so that your Father who is in heaven will also forgive you your transgressions. [But if you do not forgive, neither will your Father who is in heaven forgive your transgressions.] Mark 11:25-26 (NASB 1995)

Today it is popular to be offended, and many people are rewarded as victims for things the Bible calls sin. Some people even get their identity from being a victim. Holding on to hurt, offense, resentment or unforgiveness against God or others, causes us to have a hardened heart. The above verse says that if we do not forgive, then God will not forgive us. We have all hurt others and been hurt ourselves. It damages us and causes us to put up barriers to avoid further injury. Generally, those who hurt us are themselves wounded. Unforgiveness stops the flow of God's love to us and through us. Jesus called us to come to Him and lay our burdens at the foot of the cross (Matt 11:28). Forgiveness opens the way for healing and reconciliation.

If we confess our sins, He is faithful and just to forgive us our sins and cleanse us from all unrighteousness. 1 Jn 1:9

Dear Lord Jesus, You were killed by those who hated You and yet You forgave them. I offer You my wounded heart and choose this day to forgive those who have hurt me. Thank You for forgiving me and cleansing me. Lk 23:34; Matt 18:21-22

Week 3, Day 7: Agreement

Behold, how good and how pleasant it is for brothers to live together in unity! It is like the precious oil on the head, running down upon the beard, as on Aaron's beard, the oil which ran down upon the edge of his robes. It is like the dew of Hermon coming down upon the mountains of Zion; for the LORD commanded the blessing there – life forever. Psalm 133:1-3

We can, of course pray alone and should do this daily, but we should not neglect also praying together with others, especially as a family. Agreement is not a prerequisite but a promise of blessing. A home where the family prays together is far more likely to stay together. In a Jewish home, it is traditional at the beginning of the Sabbath for the Father to bless the wife and each of the children before eating the meal together. This bonds the family.

If a matter is of particular concern, seeking the advice of one or two trusted spiritual elders or friends will not only help share the burden but this agreement in prayer multiplies, rather than adds, power to our prayers. Prayer partners are a wonderful blessing.

Truly, truly, I say to you, if you ask the Father for anything in My name, He will give it to you. Until now you have asked for nothing in My name; ask and you will receive, so that your joy may be made full. Jn 16:23-24

Father, show me who to partner with in prayer for my own spiritual growth. Thank You that You desire to give me fullness of joy through this prayer journey.

Week 4
Agreement with God

Week 4, Day 1: The only way

And there is salvation in no one else; for there is no other name under heaven that has been given among mankind by which we must be saved.
Acts 4:12

Prayer is not just pouring out our heart's desires to God, although that is not a bad thing to do. Our hearts need to be agreeing with what God has stated in His Word and with what is on His heart, for Him to act on our prayers.

The current culture of our society believes that all gods are the same. Indigenous spirits and multiculturalism are being exalted. While the redeemed indigenous people hold a special authority in God's Kingdom, we cannot bow to pagan, animistic gods and the cultural practices that accompany them. Our minds and our spirits need renewing from the ungodly aspects of our cultures (Rom 12:1-2).

Every man-made religion seeks their god's favour by human works. We can never earn our salvation. Paul declares that 'there is none righteous…for all have sinned and fallen short of the glory of God' (Ps 14:1-3, Rom 3:10, 23). We are all guilty before the Judge of the earth and need the Saviour. Jesus alone paid the price by His sacrificial death and resurrection. He is the *only* way. We are redeemed by the blood of Jesus, not good works and no other religion. We need above all else to pray for salvation for all sinners whether atheists, agnostics, humanists, Jews, Muslims and Buddhists, or followers of any other man-made belief.

Heavenly Father, renew my mind to think as You think and let my heart be humble and malleable to your correction. Thank You, Jesus for taking the weight of sin upon yourself that I may be free and reconciled with the Father. I pray for the salvation of my family and friends.

Week 4, Day 2: The nature of sin

The Light shines in the darkness and the darkness did not overpower it.
John 1:5 (NASB 1995 margin)

Darkness is dispelled by light and darkness cannot enter where light abounds. The dark nature of sin separates us from God. We cannot enter His presence when we carry sin in our lives. When we repent, the blood of Jesus erases our dark deeds, and through Him we can come into the Father's house washed clean and clothed in righteousness. But sin breaks relationship and grieves the Father who pines for our company. We therefore need to hate the sin that causes us to hide from the presence of God as Adam and Eve did in the garden (Gen 3:8). If we love God, we will want to draw close to Him.

For our prayers to be answered we must agree with God's verdict and call sin by its name without trying to attribute it to a bygone culture. That is not popular today and may cause 'offense'. While we need to be sensitive to others, we need to be more sensitive to offending God. We can never be set free when we argue with God, and it is not loving others to cover up the danger of continuing in what the Bible calls sin. Sin is destructive and leads to death. Satan wants to steal, kill and destroy us for short term pleasure, but Jesus came to set us free for eternal life.

Dear Jesus, gently show me where I have offended You and give me courage to be a life-giver to others as well.

Week 4, Day 3: Self-justification

'For I know the plans that I have for you,' declares the LORD, 'plans for prosperity and not for disaster, to give you a future and a hope.' Jeremiah 29:11

Many people have suffered horrible physical, mental or emotional abuse in their lives, even from people who should have loved them. We will never be healed if we use past abuse as a reason for not changing our future. We have to agree with God that it is wrong to hold grudges, unforgiveness, resentment or bitterness against other people no matter what wrongs they have done to us.

Jesus forgave those who mocked, tortured and killed Him. He understands. If we feel that the other person is wrong and use that to justify our unforgiveness, we are not in a good position to see our prayers answered. It may be true, but we have to do as Jesus did and rise above that. Remember that Jesus forgave us before we even realised that we were sinners. We must ask God to help us forgive and repent of the sin of unforgiveness. God desires to set us free and bring us into a better place so He can prosper our future, not have us remain captured by the past.

In 2020, the Abdullah family lost three children and their cousin to a drunk driver who crashed into the children who were walking along the footpath to buy ice creams. The Abdullahs made a choice to forgive the driver and on the first anniversary launched 'i4give Day'[1] and have since ministered to thousands of others who have faced tragedy. God can turn a tragedy into an opportunity if we offer it to Him.

Lord Jesus, I choose this day to forgive those who have hurt and abused me. Help me to let go and let God deal with my aggressors. Matt 6:12,14-15, and the Psalms of David.

Week 4, Day 4: Self-pity

... in reference to your former manner of life, you lay aside the old self, which is being corrupted in accordance with the lusts of deceit, and that you be renewed in the spirit of your mind, and put on the new self, which in the likeness of God has been created in righteousness and holiness of the truth. Ephesians 4:22-24

I went through a period of depression which came about because God was not answering my prayers as I thought He should. I was angry and felt abandoned by God so had dug myself into a hole of misery. The Lord began to turn things around one day when He clearly spoke to me and said, 'Self-pity is a sin.' This shocked me as I had felt quite justified in my feelings! I had to agree with God, repent, ask His forgiveness and allow God to start to heal me. The situation did not change but I changed and He lovingly pulled me out of the pit and back into the daylight so I could see the situation from a different perspective. We have to get our eyes off ourselves and on to Jesus. It is a matter of crucifying the flesh.

We have all suffered rejection – some more than others – but this does not have to define who we are. We need to see ourselves as God sees us and not come under the labels that other people or circumstances have put upon us.

Father, forgive me where I have taken my eyes off You and fallen into the pit of self-pity. Help me to look to You the author and finisher of my faith. Heb 12:2

Week 4, Day 5: Health

And He said, 'If you will give earnest heed to the voice of the Lord your God, and do what is right in His sight, and give ear to His commandments, and keep all His statutes, I will put none of the diseases on you which I have put on the Egyptians; for I, the Lord, am your healer.' Exodus 15:26

It is not God's will for us to be sick in mind, body or spirit. We must believe that He is good and wants the best for us. This means spending time with Him to find the root causes of our illness, which are often spiritual, and grow in faith to believe for healing. It is often much easier to run to the doctor or pharmacy to get some medicine and sometimes the Lord will direct us to do that. We are fortunate to have this at our disposal, but our first port of call should be the Lord not the doctor. Only He can take us to the root cause and not just deal with the symptoms. The Lord desires our complete inner and outer healing, not just the superficial layer, which may return at a later date if the cause has not been addressed. We need to agree with God that He wants us to be whole and repent for unbelief.

Bless the LORD, O my soul, and all that is within me, bless His holy name. Bless the LORD, O my soul, and forget none of His benefits; who pardons all your iniquities, who heals all your diseases... Ps 103:1-3. Read Is 53:5, Matt 4:24, 8:16

Week 4, Day 6: Money

The LORD will open for you His good storehouse, the heavens, to give rain to your land in its season and to bless all the work of your hand; and you shall lend to many nations, but you shall not borrow. The LORD will make you the head and not the tail…if you listen to the commandments of the LORD your God…to follow them carefully. Deuteronomy 28:12-13

Some people have a poverty mentality or believe that the world owes them a living. One month's salary per year of every working person's income goes into social services. While there are times and situations when this is totally justified and right (the elderly and disabled), our society is far too dependent on the state to look after us instead of using our time and gifts to feed ourselves (2 Thess 3:10). It is often easier to rely on the state than rely on the Lord, but it denies us the close relationship with Him that He seeks. Unemployment is also demeaning our value instead of seeing ourselves as God sees us. We need to believe that He will provide for us and that He wants to prosper us, which may involve overcoming our fears and inferiority complex. We owe it to God and the world to use the gifts He has given us and not hide our talents under a bushel (Matt 5:15). As we are faithful in using our gifts, He will bless us and multiply our fruit (Matt 25:15).

On the other hand, affluence can be a trap if it is not managed well. We are not to hoard or lust after wealth but rather be a conduit for God's blessings to flow through us to those in need (Acts 20:35).

For the love of money is a root of all sorts of evil, and some by longing for it have wandered away from the faith and pierced themselves with many griefs. 1 Tim 6:10

Dear Lord, help me to be grateful for what You have given me, to use my talents to provide for me, my family and others, to be generous and to use my wealth wisely for your Kingdom.

Week 4, Day 7: Sexuality

Do not have sexual relations with your neighbour's wife and defile yourself with her. Do not give any of your children to be sacrificed to Molek... Do not have sexual relations with a man as one does with a woman; that is detestable. Do not have sexual relations with an animal... that is a perversion. Leviticus 18:20-21a, 22-23a,c (NIVUK)

Sexual sin is rife. Extra-marital relations are considered 'normal' especially by men, but unfaithfulness breaks down marriages and hurts partners and children. Leviticus 18:20-25 and Romans 1:18-32 show us the slippery slope from fornication and adultery, to abortion, homosexuality and bestiality with the consequence of defiling and cursing the land.

Sexual perversion is being heavily promoted in our schools. Pornography has been viewed by 85% of young people aged 14-18 which sets them up for addiction and affairs.[2] God wants our eye gate clean. Children are being brainwashed into gender confusion and parents need to be aware and stand against this manipulation. Children under 10 are being pushed into sex-changing drugs and irreversible surgery, maiming them for life.

One child in 5,000 is born with an indistinct sexuality. Deception from the gay lobby aggressively pushes the lie of people being born 'gay' and that gender is a choice. The organs we have are what God meant us to be. We can only be healed by agreeing that God did not make a mistake when He created us (Ps 139). Good models of masculinity or femininity are desperately needed since gender dysphoria is often based in family breakdown or abuse. In Ezekiel 16:49-50, God pinpoints the root of sodomy as arrogance, haughtiness (pride), abundance and not helping the less fortunate (selfish indulgence).

Father, forgive us for dishonouring You in our bodies and causing ourselves, others and especially children to be hurt or stray from You by our actions. Rom 1:18-32; Lev 18:20f

Week 5
Alignment with God

Week 5, Day 1: In Christ

Gideon was beating out wheat in the wine press in order to save it from the Midianites. And the angel of the LORD appeared to him and said to him, 'The LORD is with you, valiant warrior.' Judges 6:11-12

Gideon was living in fear and felt He was the least qualified of His tribe to be a warrior, but God saw him differently. Moses argued that he could not speak well (Ex 4:10). David was not considered worthy by his father to even be presented to the prophet, but God had chosen him to be a king (1 Sam 16). Jonah was called by God to go to the wicked city of Nineveh but immediately ran the other way! Jeremiah thought he was too young (Jer 1:6) and Abraham thought he was too old (Gen 18:11).

God looks at the heart not the impossible human condition. He seeks not for our abilities but our availability. Nothing is impossible to Him, and we just need to be obedient when He calls. When He asks us to do something, He will provide all that is needed and will never leave us nor forsake us in the process (Heb 13:5). We just have to align our will to His and walk with Him to see the miracles unfold and victory over every impossibility.

Heavenly Father, I choose to make myself available for your purposes. Use me as You desire. Help me not to make excuses but to be quick to say 'Yes and Amen' when You call me.

Week 5, Day 2: On God's side

Now it came about when Joshua was by Jericho…and behold, a man was standing opposite him with his sword drawn…and Joshua…said to him, 'Are you for us or for our enemies?' He said, "No; rather I have come now as captain of the army of the LORD." Joshua 5:13-14

The angel (or Jesus himself) was not buying into Joshua's mindset to take sides. He was sent from God and was there to fulfil God's agenda alone. We often try to get God on our side, especially when asking Him to deal with those who are being difficult, but God is fulfilling His purposes, not ours. His angels and servants obey His voice. We need to let go of our opinions, biases and pre-conceived ideas and get on His side. God's armies will fight for us when we are aligned to His will and about His Kingdom business.

'For My thoughts are not your thoughts, nor are your ways My ways,' declares the LORD. 'For as the heavens are higher than the earth, so are My ways higher than your ways and My thoughts than your thoughts.' Is 55:8-9

Agreement is of the mind but alignment is action and deeds. To align with God, we need to submit to the higher thoughts that are not based on a worldly paradigm and avoid trying to do things in a humanistic way. God's ways are supernatural and mostly different to human reason, and therefore He will receive the glory and be known to us and others.

Lord, I lay down my pre-conceived ideas and biased opinions in order for You to reveal your higher thoughts and perfect ways.

Week 5, Day 3: Understanding God's plans

Therefore, many other signs Jesus also performed in the presence of the disciples, which are not written in this book; but these have been written so that you may believe that Jesus is the Christ, the Son of God; and that believing you may have life in His name. John 20:30-31

God's Word is not written as a science textbook but chiefly so that we might believe and move from the kingdom of darkness and death into the Kingdom of light and life. God's purposes are for salvation, redemption and restoration, and we are to continue the work of Jesus on earth.

Truly, truly, I say to you, he who believes in Me, the works that I do, he will do also; and greater works than these he will do; because I go to the Father. Jn 14:12

Jesus did mighty works while on earth but promises us even greater ones in the power of the Spirit. Can we believe for these? What or who is it that God wants to use you to save, redeem or restore? God's individual plan for us will always align with the global plan of the Scriptures. It is only a matter of finding our place within that wider framework. We also need to understand His ways – the way of surrender and sacrifice. Our task is to lay our lives down so that others can come into His Kingdom and find life.

Lord, make me willing to lay down my will so that your will can be done through me.

Week 5, Day 4: The way of the cross

Then Jesus said to His disciples, 'If anyone wants to come after Me, he must deny himself, take up his cross, and follow Me.' Matthew 16:24

Alignment has a cost. Salvation is free but to walk with the Lord will cost us everything. In a world of attention-getting Facebook likes, huge profit-oriented business gimmicks and advertising targeted to lure our sensual lusts and pride, it goes against the grain to be told we must deny ourselves.

For all that is in the world, the lust of the flesh and the lust of the eyes and the boastful pride of life, is not from the Father, but is from the world. 1 Jn 2:16

The world's definition of success is having lots of earthly possessions, influence and a big name. The only thing that counts in God's Kingdom is obedience. Our pride, ambitions, lusts and selfishness must go on the altar. The Lord cannot fill up a glass that is already full of our own desires. To be directed, we need to make room for Him. We are told to follow Him, not for Him to just fulfil our needs. Where is He moving today? He will always be there for us but we are meant primarily to be there for Him. We are His creation and belong to Him for His pleasure and service. Our success is when we see His Kingdom come through our obedience. Alignment means that we are willing to lay aside our plans and desires in order to fulfil God's plans and desires.

Lord, show me where I need to make more room for You to come and dwell with me. Teach me the way of the cross.

Week 5, Day 5: Advancing the Kingdom

Jesus was going through all the cities and villages, teaching in their synagogues and proclaiming the gospel of the kingdom, and healing every disease and every sickness. Matthew 9:35

The gospel Jesus preached was the gospel of the Kingdom of God not the gospel of salvation, although salvation is the first step by which we enter the Kingdom. The full gospel involves bringing God's Kingdom reign on earth as it is in heaven. It is much broader than filling churches with converts. Converts need to walk with Jesus and take His rulership into their homes, workplaces, streets, and every sector of society. For this we need the five-fold ministries to be operating and to change our paradigm of 'church'. There is more on this in later sections.

This gospel of the kingdom shall be preached in the whole world as a testimony to all the nations, and then the end will come. Matt 24:14

The true preaching of the gospel releases signs and wonders. Jesus promised miracles would accompany the believers, and it all starts with prayer.

These signs will accompany those who have believed: in My name they will cast out demons, they will speak with new tongues…they will lay hands on the sick, and they will recover. Mk 16:17-18

Heavenly Father, change my thinking to believe that You want to do miracles not only of salvation but also signs and wonders through me. Teach me to pray in expectation and faith.

Week 5, Day 6: Finding our place

You will receive power when the Holy Spirit has come upon you; and you shall be My witnesses both in Jerusalem and in all Judea, and Samaria, and as far as the remotest part of the earth. Acts 1:8

Testifying about Jesus in our words and our actions is a general and global call for all believers. To do this effectively, we need the power of the Holy Spirit to fill us to overflowing. We cannot do it without Him. Within that general purpose, we need God's guidance to find the specific people He will lead us to, and how to reach them.

Not everyone is gifted as an evangelist. Some have a gift of compassion that draws people to share their hearts and problems. This is an opportunity to pray with them and for them. Others may have a servant heart that is happy to help with practical work. As you serve the Lord in this way, He will open doors to share the love of God. Perhaps you have a gift of hospitality and enjoy entertaining. Use that to also share your faith. We do not all have to be up-front preachers or leaders. Most churches are crying out for people to help with the technological aspects of a service or with the children.

If you want to learn more about prayer, take every opportunity to talk to and pray alongside those in your church, homegroup or online who are more experienced. Numerous online prayer meetings have sprung up which are praying regularly for international, national, or regional issues. There is much online teaching available now, so just search your area of interest.

Dear Lord, please fill me afresh with your Holy Spirit that I may witness effectively for You. Show me who to talk to about You. Open doors that no one can shut. 1 Cor 12, 1 Cor 16:9

Week 5, Day 7: Watching and waiting

She [Anna] did not leave the temple grounds, serving night and day with fasts and prayers. And at that very moment she came up and began giving thanks to God, and continued to speak about Him to all those who were looking forward to the redemption of Jerusalem. Luke 2:37-38

Anna was an elderly widow who had her heart focussed on God. She was fasting and praying in the temple and prophesied about Jesus (Lk 2:36-38). She was in the right place at the right time to testify to who Jesus was. Simeon was most likely a retired priest. He knew the Law and was in the temple waiting for Jesus (Lk 2:21-35). He was 'righteous and devout, looking for the consolation of Israel and the Holy Spirit was upon him' (v. 25), even before Pentecost! He recognised the baby Jesus as the Messiah and declared His prophetic destiny.

Knowing the 'what' of God in a situation is the beginning of the journey, not the end of the story. We need to be careful not to fall into presumption and run eagerly off in our own strength to do what we believe God has said. After the 'what', then wait for the 'where', 'when', 'how' and 'who with'. In the process the Lord refines our character.

Our prayers should not be driven by reacting to the negative things around us. Rather, as we watch and wait to see what the Father is doing, we will be aligning ourselves with God's will, as Jesus did. This is what should dictate our walk.

Abba Father, show me where You are working. I choose to focus on this and not all the negative things around me. Let me be a positive influence and bringer of hope where there is despair.

Week 6
Discipline of prayer

Week 6, Day 1: An imperishable prize

And He came to the disciples and found them sleeping, and He said to Peter, 'So, you men could not keep watch with Me for one hour?' Matthew 26:40

A dear friend of mine was crying out to God and asking why we do not see the miracles today that were common in the New Testament. God's answer to her was, 'Because you pray when you feel like it, not in a disciplined way'. Ouch! How many of us fall into this category?

If we want to see the greater works and have our prayers answered, we need to generate some self-discipline. This is not popular in a self-seeking, do-what-feels-good, buy-now-pay-later culture. But in the end, we all know that we have to put in the hard yards if we want to see results. No Olympic athlete wins a prize without much sacrifice and many years of training. Swimmers are up at 5 am, train for a few hours, go to school and are back in the pool again after school.

Everyone who competes in the games, exercises self-control in all things. So they do it to obtain a perishable wreath, but we an imperishable. 1 Cor 9:25

It is worth the effort to develop a disciplined prayer life. The prize we will attain is far greater than an Olympic medal. It is imperishable and eternal.

Holy Spirit, come stir my heart to desire God's presence above all else and fill me with your power to overcome the flesh.

Week 6, Day 2: Crucifying the flesh

And in the early morning, while it was still dark, Jesus got up, left the house, and went away to a secluded place, and prayed there for a time. Mark 1:35

The best time to meet with God is to put Him first in the morning so He can direct our day. Try to find a quiet place and consistent time. Turn off the phone and minimise distractions. If you have a small baby that wakes you up at 4 or 5am for a feed, then choose a time when the baby is asleep. If you are a tradie that begins the day at 7am and has to travel an hour and a half to get there, then put in the ear plugs on the train or put worship music on in the car rather than the radio. (Just keep your eyes open as you drive and pray!)

But the fruit of the Spirit is love, joy, peace, patience, kindness, goodness, faithfulness, gentleness, self-control; against such things there is no law. Now those who belong to Christ Jesus crucified the flesh with its passions and desires. Gal 5:22-24

Discipline is a fruit of the Spirit that is developed over time, together with other character attributes as we crucify the flesh and allow the Holy Spirit to flood more and more of our lives. Trying to keep the law or control our passions and desires in our own strength is not generally profitable, but that is why God has sent us His Spirit. As we yield to Him, He will make God's desires our own and we will find joy in Him that overrides our flesh.

Dear Lord, give me the desires that are on your heart. Plant the fruit of the Spirit in my heart and water them daily so I become more like You.

Week 6, Day 3: Adding Character

Now for this very reason also, applying all diligence, in your faith supply moral excellence, and in your moral excellence, knowledge, and in your knowledge, self-control, and in your self-control, perseverance, and in your perseverance, godliness, and in your godliness, brotherly kindness, and in your brotherly kindness, love. 2 Peter 1:5-7

Our prayer life must be backed up by a lifestyle of godly character. People are very quick to see inconsistencies between what we say and what we do. The Pharisees were faithful in religious prayer, tithing and fasting, and many Jews today are still very disciplined in their prayer, but it is mostly based in repeating prayers of past rabbis from the Sidur (prayer book) which includes many psalms from the Scriptures. While this is good and keeps the focus off praying self-centred prayers, Jesus was critical of their lifestyle that lacked the love of God towards people and led to judgmentalism and arrogance (Rom 10:3). He was far more moved by the penitent prayer of the despised tax collector than the long prayers of the religious aristocracy (Lk 18:9-14).

It is the prayers of the heart that build relationship with the Father. Faith rises as we know Him more and experience His character. His character is then imputed to us and we become clothed with His righteousness.

I will rejoice greatly in the LORD, my soul will be joyful in my God; for He has clothed me with garments of salvation, He has wrapped me with a robe of righteousness, as a groom puts on a turban, and as a bride adorns herself with her jewels. Is 61:10

Abba Father, help me to pray prayers from my heart that will touch your heart. Show me your character and mould my character to reflect yours.

Week 6, Day 4: Broken walls

Like a city that is broken into and without walls, so is a person who has no self-control over his spirit. Proverbs 25:28

Disciplined prayer builds walls of protection around our life. A former work colleague used to have a sign on her desk that said, 'The main thing is to keep the main thing the main thing'. Distractions are always lurking around us. Learning to prioritise, especially in our spiritual life, is so important. We are to seek first the Kingdom of God, so that He can supply all our other needs (Matt 6:33).

Turning to Him first in every situation can become as natural as breathing if we constantly practise this and don't allow panic or fear to take hold. Our worst enemy is the busyness of life that wants to grab our time to do all the 'urgent' things that we or others want to impose on us. That is where discipline comes in and the ability to set priorities and stick to them. We need to learn to say no to some things that we or others may want us to do. It is a continual choice to put God first. It takes an average of about 66 days for a new habit to become automatic so in a couple of months our new discipline can be established. Of course, we will have to contend with the devil to overcome him and our own flesh to set a new course for our life. But it will be worth it.

Dear Lord, help me to make good choices today that put your Kingdom first and not allow myself to be pulled aside by the world's priorities.

Week 6, Day 5: Pray without ceasing

Rejoice always, pray without ceasing, in everything give thanks; for this is the will of God for you in Christ Jesus. 1 Thessalonians 5:16-18

How do we pray without ceasing when we have all the things of life to deal with? We have to work, study, shop, wash, deal with the family, change nappies etc. It seems an impossibility.

For My house will be called a house of prayer for all the peoples. Is 56:7

The temple was intended to be a house of prayer for all nations, but became defiled by corrupt priests. Our bodies are now the temple of the Holy Spirit (1 Cor 6:19). As we abide in Christ and He abides in us, we become a house of prayer remaining God-conscious throughout the day (Jn 15:4-5). Furthermore, it is the body of Christ that is called to be a house of prayer.

You also, as living stones, are being built up as a spiritual house for a holy priesthood, to offer spiritual sacrifices that are acceptable to God through Jesus Christ. 1 Pet 2:5

Peter likens the body of believers to living stones which together make up the New Testament temple of God. Perhaps we are not meant to be this house of prayer alone? If a group of believers becomes a unified organic body in a region, we can be praying without ceasing as a 24/7 house of prayer.

Dear Lord, You were a walking house of prayer on the earth. As I abide in You and You remain with me, make me into a house of prayer as You are.

Week 6, Day 6: Pray in the Spirit

With every prayer and request, pray at all times in the Spirit. Ephesians 6:18a

Our prayers are meant to be prayers in the Spirit, not in the flesh. They must stem from heaven not earth. Praying in tongues will be dealt with later but this is also an effective way to walk in prayer. We do not then have to engage the conscious mind as we are praying spirit to Spirit.

But the Helper, the Holy Spirit whom the Father will send in My name, He will teach you all things, and remind you of all that I said to you. Jn 14:26

The Holy Spirit will also bring things to our remembrance. When He prompts us to look at a scripture, brings a picture of someone into our mind or lays a burden on our heart, then run with it. Look up the scripture and ask for more revelation. Pray for the person of whom He has reminded you. Ask the Lord for how to pray for them. Ask for a word of encouragement to give them. Pray into the situation the Lord has given you a burden for. Ask the Holy Spirit to help you. This type of prayer and waiting should not replace the disciplined reading of the Bible as we need to get the Word into our spirits first, so that the Holy Spirit can remind us of a verse, an event or biblical character to follow up.

A major work of the Holy Spirit is to bring conviction of sin (Jn 16:8). When praying for salvation for someone, pray for the Spirit to soften their heart and make them receptive to the gospel message. The Holy Spirit will also guide us to truth (Jn 16:13) and testify to who Jesus is (Jn 15:26).

Father, I am asking You for revelation today by your Holy Spirit. Breathe life into the Scriptures and lead my prayers.

Week 6, Day 7: Be alert

But stay alert at all times, praying that you will have strength to escape all these things that are going to take place, and to stand before the Son of Man. Luke 21:36

We are living in the end of the 'end times.' When we read the prophecies of Luke chapter 21 and Matthew chapter 24, we see so much of that happening in our day. We desperately need to be hearing from the Holy Spirit. Deception is all around us and rapidly increasing with Artificial Intelligence mimicking reality. We cannot trust what is sent to us by email, as wicked people are trying to steal our identity to scam us of our life's savings. Christian beliefs are no longer accepted, and often actively opposed, in our education and health systems. Doctors and teachers are threatened if they promote biblical practices of health and life. Lawlessness abounds (1 Thess 2). Persecution is increasing. Only disciplined prayer will keep us alert to the Lord's promptings.

Jesus warns us to be ready, praying for strength in these times. We may be whisked away in the rapture or be called to stand and witness before kings. We need to be prepared for either. The first disciples were told to leave Jerusalem when soldiers surrounded it (Lk 21:20-21)! That is impossible but the siege was stopped when the emperor died, so they could escape. However, Christians are being martyred daily in numerous countries of the world just because of their faith in Jesus.

Loving Jesus, I pray for discernment, wisdom and courage to hold strongly to You in the face of persecution. Let me not cower if intimidated, flee in fear or ever deny You. Strengthen my faith to love my enemies as You did.

Week 7
Obedience

Week 7, Day 1: Choices

The LORD God commanded the man, saying, 'From any tree of the garden you may freely eat; but from the tree of the knowledge of good and evil you shall not eat, for on the day that you eat from it you will certainly die.' Genesis 2:16-17

God did not create robots. In the garden of Eden (meaning 'pleasure'), He created humans and gave them freewill so they could choose to love Him. Love can only exist where there is freedom. *Adam* in Hebrew means humankind and the Hebrew today for a human being is *ben adam* or son of Adam. Adam was not just one man but represents the collective human race. Adam and Eve were only given one command and warned that disobedience would result in death: not death from poisonous fruit but death of a free, loving relationship with their Creator. Their choice is also ours: choose life by obedience to God's instructions or independence from God, the way of man, leading to death. Do I surrender to God or go my own way?

The heart is more deceitful than all else and is desperately sick; who can understand it? Jer 17:9

Adam blamed Eve and she blamed the serpent. The result was that they were cast out of the garden to save them from remaining in that fallen state for eternity. It meant toil and hardship in place of God's provision. Our choices begin by taking responsibility for our actions and not shifting the blame to others.

Dear Lord, my natural inclination is to want to do things my own way and choose the wrong fruit. Show me where I am blaming others and not taking responsibility. I choose You this day.

Week 7, Day 2: Blessings of obedience

...If you diligently obey the LORD your God, being careful to do all His commandments which I command you today, the LORD your God will set you high above all the nations of the earth. All these blessings will come upon you and overtake you if you obey the LORD your God. Deuteronomy 28:1-2 (NASB 1995)

The following verses outline a long list of blessings that follow obedience. God gave us the law (literally 'instructions') not to curb our freedom but to give us a handbook to blessing for our lives. The Mosaic law was a constitution given to the fledgling nation that had just escaped from 400 years of slavery, so had little idea how to function as a nation. Every nation needs a constitution to maintain justice and social order. Israel's was given directly from heaven. It included moral law inscribed on the tablets in the ten commandments, social law which governed things like reparation for damages, economic provision, and ceremonial law.

The law shows us our own sinful nature. When we know the law and then break it, we realise our guilt and need for a saviour. Jesus took the law right back to the root in the heart rather than the actual action of sin. He came to fulfil the law not do away with it (Matt 5:17). He completed the sacrifice for sin so animal sacrifice is no longer needed. However, we are still to walk out our salvation with fear and trembling in sanctification (Philippians 2:12). The law in the New Covenant is written on our hearts, not on stone, and the Holy Spirit has been sent to help us with our walk.

Father, cleanse me of all unrighteousness and cause me to walk in the truth of your blessings. Are we lawbreakers? Read Matthew chapters 5 to 7.

Week 7, Day 3: Curses of disobedience

If you do not obey the LORD your God, to be careful to follow all His commandments and His statutes which I am commanding you today, then all these curses will come upon you and overtake you. Deuteronomy 28:15

A quick read of the curses outlined in the rest of this long chapter should put the fear of God into any person. The list includes chronic disease, mental illness and confusion, drought, plagues, lack of productivity, theft, destruction and servitude, severe hunger, loss of inheritance, cities being besieged and the people being driven from the land. Much of this has indeed come upon the Jewish people as they have forsaken the Lord. Who would choose this life of devastation? Yet we do every time we make wrong choices and follow our fleshly lusts. Thank God for His patience towards us and His redemptive power to bring us back.

The more we learn to listen and obey the promptings of the Holy Spirit and understand His book of instructions, the more we will avoid the pitfalls that can have long-term consequences and destroy our lives. As our Western nations are choosing to cast aside the Bible and its teachings, we are seeing more and more families falling apart, children committing suicide and lawlessness and crime abounding. Turning our backs on God's instructions not only affects individuals but also nations. Let us be quick to repent.

If we confess our sins, He is faithful and righteous, so that He will forgive us our sins and cleanse us from all unrighteousness. 1 Jn 1:9

Meditate on Psalm 119 and the value King David put on the Word of God.

Week 7, Day 4: The cost of obedience

'We gave you strict orders not to continue teaching in this name, and yet you have filled Jerusalem with your teaching and intend to bring this Man's blood upon us.' But Peter and the apostles answered, "We must obey God rather than men." Acts 5:28-29

When God calls us to an assignment or mission, it will normally be far too big for us to do and will require much prayer, faith and obedience to accomplish. Peter and John were filled with the Holy Spirit at Pentecost and, as they were commanded, went about preaching and healing the sick with great authority and success. It did not take long for this to arouse the ire and jealousy of the religious leaders who wanted to retain their power over the people. They had them flogged and thrown into prison. The apostles were eventually released and ordered not to preach in Jesus' name but they could not obey an order than conflicted with Jesus' command.

We will also have to choose not to bow to human demands and possibly 'offend' some people (as Jesus did) or stand for truth and obey God. Do we want God's blessing or human approval?

Nevertheless many, even of the rulers, believed in Him, but because of the Pharisees they were not confessing Him, so that they would not be excommunicated from the synagogue; for they loved the approval of people rather than the approval of God. Jn 12:42-43

Following Jesus will cost us, as the world will try to pull us back into its ways and being 'normal' in its eyes. We have to choose to be different but 'salty'.

Dear Lord, help me to choose the approval of God over the approval of men and be obedient to your call whatever the cost. Prov 29:25

Week 7, Day 5: The cost of disobedience

But whoever denies Me before people, I will also deny him before My Father who is in heaven. Matthew 10:33

Obedience is costly – but then so is disobedience. We saw the horrific curses for disobedience. If we think the road of obedience is too hard and want to camp where life is more comfortable or even turn our back on God, there is also a cost. God turns His face away from us, together with His blessings, and we reap the fruit of our choices. All our actions have consequences for good or for bad. Bad choices have negative consequences, sometimes life-changing. If we have once tasted of the goodness of God, then turned away, it becomes even harder than at first to find our way back (but for the grace of God).

For it is impossible, in the case of those who have once been enlightened and have tasted of the heavenly gift and have been made partakers of the Holy Spirit, and have tasted the good word of God and the powers of the age to come, and then have fallen away, to restore them again to repentance, since they again crucify to themselves the Son of God and put Him to open shame. Heb 6:4-6

If we want God to continue speaking to us and communicating with us, then we must keep walking in obedience and not look back.

Jesus replied, 'No one who puts a hand to the plough and looks back is fit for service in the kingdom of God.' Lk 9:62 (NIVUK)

Heavenly Father, give me courage and faith to fix my eyes on the way ahead that You have set before me and not look back to the past.

Week 7, Day 6: Generational curses

You shall not bow down to them [idols] or worship them; for I, the LORD your God, am a jealous God, punishing the children for the sin of the parents to the third and fourth generation of those who hate me, but showing love to a thousand generations of those who love me and keep my commandments. Deuteronomy 5:9-10 (NIV)

We can be afflicted with curses from our family lines. If we or our predecessors have been involved in witchcraft, idolatry, Freemasonry, bloodshed (including abortion), deviant sexuality, or false covenants, we need to close the doors that have given access to demonic spirits and be set free and released from the curses that follow. This is not to be taken lightly, and it is recommended to pray through these things with a counsellor or mature Christian.

Jesus acknowledged the demonic realm and drove out many demons. While we must focus on Jesus and not on what Satan is doing, we do need to evict him from our lives, our houses and our families. The doors are shut through repentance and turning away from these practices. Make sure to burn or remove any objects or souvenirs used for idol worship from the home and garden (e.g. Buddha statues). Ask Jesus to fill the empty places with His presence. Lately tattoos have become popular but the Bible forbids this (Lev 19:28). If you have these, especially any demonic figures, repent and ask the Lord to remove all their power. Jesus' power is much greater and Satan has been defeated on the cross (Col 2:13-15; Mk 16:17-18; Lk 10:19).

Father, I repent for myself and my ancestors for any idolatry or demonic practices and cut their influence off myself and my family. Please fill us with your Holy Spirit and your presence.

Week 7, Day 7: God's order

However, each one of you also must love his wife as he loves himself, and the wife must respect her husband. Children, obey your parents in the Lord, for this is right. 'Honour your father and mother' – which is the first commandment with a promise – 'so that it may go well with you and that you may enjoy long life on the earth.' Ephesians 5:33-6:3 (NIVUK)

God has an order to which we are to submit. We are not only to obey God, but we are to place ourselves voluntarily under His societal order. He has made the man the head of the family to love his wife and children. He has given apostles and prophets to lead the church on earth. Workers are to serve and obey their bosses and we are to honour our governmental leaders, pray for them and pay our dues (Rom 13:1-7, 1 Tim 2:1-4, Eph 5:33-6:9).

This is often where the rubber hits the road with our rebellious spirits. Submission does not come easily but this does not mean to accept an abusive situation nor to tolerate Jezebel's spirit of control, manipulation and domination. It does however, mean dealing with our own attitudes, not demanding our own way, being willing to be wrong, not bickering, gossiping, demeaning, spreading dissention or undermining the authority of those in charge. Our job is to pray and obey (even if we do not agree) but also to be peacemakers (Matt 5:9, Rom 12:18).

Dear Lord, help me to submit myself to the authorities You have set over me without complaining and to pray for those above me. May I be one who encourages them instead of criticising and offer positive answers that promote harmony.

Week 8

Repentance and prayer

Week 8, Day 1: Repent

'Brothers, what shall we do?' Peter replied, 'Repent and be baptised, every one of you, in the name of Jesus Christ for the forgiveness of your sins. And you will receive the gift of the Holy Spirit. Acts 2:37c-38 (NIVUK)

Learning to repent is an essential part of prayer for ourselves, our families, our regions and our countries. It is not a popular topic today, as the world does not want to acknowledge that God has standards and calls certain behaviour sinful which demands a response of repentance. This is offensive to those who love darkness rather than light (Jn 3:19-20) and the world tells us we must not offend anyone, even though people took offense at Jesus (Mk 6:3, Lk 7:23). It is more acceptable today to encourage people to embrace a loving Jesus but not mention repentance and turning from sin. Consequently, there is tolerance of sin and much mixture in the church. Any condemnation of even what the Bible calls an abomination is labelled 'unloving'. Hence the church has little power and is often indistinguishable from the world, leading many astray.

For the word of the cross is foolishness to those who are perishing, but to us who are being saved it is the power of God. 1 Cor 1:18

The power of God follows the true preaching of the gospel which begins with repentance. The fruit of repentance (a changed life) must be evident to confirm a true conversion. We need to return to the necessity and power of the cross in our evangelism, preaching and counselling to set people free from sin and change lives.

Lord, help me to preach a true gospel, not afraid to name sin and call people to repentance.

Week 8, Day 2: John the Baptist

And he came into all the region around the Jordan, preaching a baptism of repentance for the forgiveness of sins. Luke 3:3

The message of John the Baptist was one of repentance. Before salvation can come, repentance is essential. The Jews were relying on their heritage to make them acceptable to God. Some today also rely on the fact that they have grown up in the church, rather than having had a personal encounter with God. John demanded the fruits of repentance in Luke 3:7-14 so the axe would not destroy the tree for lack of godly fruit. As Christian teaching, even the ten commandments, has been taken out of schools, courts and government, a whole generation is not even conscious of sin and God's instructions and standards for their lives. Children are sucked into rebellion, sexual perversion, drugs and the pursuit of money that can never satisfy. The seduction of the lust of the eyes and the flesh are pushed before our eyes even if we try to avoid this. As a result, society lacks hope, and suicide is a major problem for the youth.

Before we can pray for others or our cities, we have to seek the Lord for the things in our culture that we have absorbed as 'normal' that are not 'normal' in God's Kingdom. These may be acts or just mindsets. We may not have ever even thought of these as wrong, as they are what everybody around us accepts, does and thinks. Our minds need to be renewed into Kingdom culture (Rom 12:1-2).

Father, search my heart and mind this day for old ways or thoughts that I need to change.

Week 8, Day 3: Psalm 51

Create in me a clean heart, God, and renew a steadfast spirit within me.
Psalm 51:10

Psalm 51 is the heartfelt prayer of a repentant sinner. King David abused his position as king (2 Sam 11) and allowed the lust of his eyes to desire Bathsheba then the lust of his flesh to consume his passion. She became pregnant. Things got worse as David tried to cover up his sin, and he ended up committing murder to get rid of her righteous husband. In the end, his sin also cost him the life of his own son (2 Sam 12). The repercussions of sin can be immense, but thankfully God's grace is even greater.

David knew he could not hide after the prophet, Nathan, confronted him. He acknowledged his sin against God (Ps 51:3), God's righteous judgement of his sin (v.4), his sinful nature (v.5), his need for cleansing (v.2), God's requirement of truth (v.6), God's ability to purify him and restore (v.7-9), his own inability to fix his sinful heart (v.10), his need for deliverance from the guilty verdict (v.14), that sacrifice could not take away his sin (v.16) and that God desires a broken spirit and a contrite heart (v.17). He also appeals to God's grace (v.1) and has confidence that God can and will forgive him and blot out the record of his sin (v.2, 7, 9). He prays for restoration (v.11-12) and pledges to praise God and make His salvation known (v.13-15). Wow, that is complete repentance, which God, of course, accepted. What an example for us.

We cannot fix our nature by our own efforts. We need the Holy Spirit to do His work in our heart (v.11). If we can emulate the humility of David in our prayers, we will soon find God working miracles in our lives and in our prayers.

Pray through Psalm 51 today and let God do a deep work within your heart.

Week 8, Day 4: Sowing and reaping

Do not be deceived, God is not mocked; for whatever a person sows, this he will also reap. Galatians 6:7

There are principles in God's Kingdom, most of which are the reverse of those of the world. For example, we must die to self in order to live for Christ, and leaders are called to serve not be served. Nevertheless, one principle that is true for both, is that we will generally reap what we sow. If we sow good seed, we will reap a good harvest. Our sinful actions have consequences that may need to be worked out or recompensed. The grace of God can override this, but sometimes we need to learn the hard way.

We mostly learn our life patterns from our parents. If we have godly parents, they will instil good values in us. However, many of us are not so blessed and need to learn Kingdom values. If there are repeated patterns in families, like people dying young, being 'accident prone' or having failed marriages, it is worth doing some research and asking the Lord for discernment. Also in our personal lives, the same sins may keep recurring. If the Lord shows you a root, like He did for David in 2 Sam 21:1-6, then this must be dealt with. Hopefully the restitution will not be as dramatic. Innocent bloodshed must be atoned for, but Jesus has paid the price for that, so we apply His blood to the situation.

Abba Father, show me where there are any situations in me or my family line that need action. I repent and cut off this sinful pattern from my life and ask You to fill the void with your Spirit.

Week 8, Day 5: Breaking curses

Do not turn to mediums or spiritists; do not seek them out to be defiled by them. I am the LORD your God. Leviticus 19:31

God is a God of covenant and takes covenants very seriously. Covenant breaking leaves a curse. There are generational curses that play out if we, our parents or ancestors have been involved in witchcraft, divination, idolatry, seances, palm-reading or other occult practices including Freemasonry. If you or family members have been involved in any occult or witchcraft practices, repent and cut off any association with these. Call in the Holy Spirit to fill the empty places and ask for blessing to come where the curse has been. Pray for the blood of Jesus to cover yourself, your family, your house, your car, your pets and possessions. If you have anything in the house that is associated with these practices, including indigenous worship artifacts, clear them out of your house, and command the spirits associated with them to leave.

Curses can go for several generations, so this cleanout needs to go back three or four generations. You can repent on behalf of family members (even if deceased) to break these strongholds. They will continue through a family line until broken and therefore we need to cut these ties in the spiritual realm so we can be set free. Illness or financial poverty can also result from curses. Praise God that the name of Jesus is the Name above all names and His blood shed on the cross has broken the power of all demonic powers.

Lord, I repent for myself and my family for any casual or conscious delving into the occult world. In the name of Jesus, I break all generational curses, occult or witchcraft influences off myself, I turn away from anything associated with these, dedicate myself afresh to Jesus and ask that His blood will cover these sins and wash me and my family clean. Thank You, Lord.

Week 8, Day 6: Prepare the way

Behold, I am going to send you Elijah the prophet before the coming of the great and terrible day of the LORD. Malachi 4:5

In this verse, the prophet Malachi prophesied that Elijah would come before the Messiah. Jesus declared that John the Baptist was the one sent in the spirit of Elijah to precede His earthly ministry (Matt 11:14). The calling of John was to prepare the way of the Lord (through calling people to repent) to 'give to His people the knowledge of salvation by the forgiveness of their sins' (Lk 1:77). It is also our calling as intercessors – to prepare the way for the return of the Lord as King. We do this by witnessing for the Lord, reaching out to others who do not yet know Him, by our prayer and intercessory ministry and just by being His light in the darkness.

In Peter's second sermon in Acts 3, he presents his case that Jesus has suffered to fulfil what the prophets had foretold and that He would remain in heaven 'until the period of restoration of all things, about which God spoke by the mouths of His holy prophets from ancient times' (Acts 3:21).

It is our calling as intercessors to search the Scriptures to find what has yet to be fulfilled of the promises made by the prophets and to join the heavenly armies to pray those into being. In doing so, we are preparing the way for the Lord's return.

Dear Lord Jesus, show me the things that still need to be fulfilled from your Word that I may join in preparing the way for your return.

Week 8, Day 7: But they refused to repent

And the people were scorched with fierce heat; and they blasphemed the name of God who has the power over these plagues, and they did not repent so as to give Him glory. Revelation 16:9

We live in a post-Christian era when the governments and nations are turning against God, and consequently, lawlessness and rebellion are rising rapidly. Judgement is coming in the form of wars, diseases, earthquakes, tsunamis, fires, floods and plagues. The world may blame climate change, China, Israel, government error or agricultural mismanagement, but in the end, God is allowing these things because of rampant sin. In the midst of these disasters, He is calling for our attention and for us as individuals to repent and to intercede for our nations.

The saddest verse in the whole of Scripture for me is, '*and they refused to repent*'. Judgement starts in the house of God but does not end there.

For it is time for judgement to begin at the household of God; and if it begins with us, what will be the outcome for those who do not obey the gospel of God? 1 Pet 4:17 (ESVUK)

The disgraceful sexual sins of the church are being revealed to the world. For this we must repent. But pornography, marriage breakups, tolerance of other gods, blasphemy etc. are also widespread in our churches. The church, as well as our nation, is ripe for God's judgement but a pure, praying, humble, repentant ecclesia is the answer for the world.

For I am not ashamed of the gospel, for it is the power of God for salvation to everyone who believes, to the Jew first and also to the Greek. Rom 1:16

Father, make me a part of the answer and not a part of the problem.

Week 9

Prayer and fasting

Week 9, Day 1: When you fast

Now whenever you fast, do not make a gloomy face as the hypocrites do, for they distort their faces so that they will be noticed by people when they are fasting. Truly I say to you, they have their reward in full. Matthew 6:16

Fasting is a generally neglected practice in the church today. We justify our neglect with all manner of spiritual or nutritional excuses, but basically, we are not willing to sacrifice our appetites in order to bring God glory, prevail in prayer, break through spiritual barriers and pay the cost required to see the Kingdom of God established in our own lives and beyond. But a person committed to prayer needs to learn this discipline.

In the Sermon on the Mount, Jesus said 'When you give…when you pray…when you fast…' (Matt 6:2,5,16). It was not 'if', but 'when'. It is clear from this that giving, praying and fasting were all accepted and assumed practices by Jesus' audience. Anna not only prayed in the temple but also fasted (Lk 2:37), as did the righteous Pharisees (Matt 9:14, Lk 18:12). Jesus fasted before His ministry began (Lk 4:1-13) and Paul sought the Lord with fasting in Acts 13:1-3 and 14:23. While the disciples were with Jesus, they did not fast because the Bridegroom was among them, but He assumed they would again do so after He departed (Matt 9:14-15).

Heavenly Father, teach me to put aside my fleshly needs and be willing to fast when and how You ask me to. Teach me how to fast to know You better.

Week 9, Day 2: Why fast?

Consecrate a fast, proclaim a solemn assembly; Gather the elders and all the inhabitants of the land to the house of the LORD your God, and cry out to the LORD. Joel 1:14

In the book of Joel, the land was overrun by a plague of locusts and/or physical armies. God called the priests and the elders to His house to repent, fast and weep before Him for deliverance. Fasting is a sign of humility and mourning for sin, sharing God's hatred for sin (Jonah 3:5,10). Fasting is also associated with sorrow for death (2 Sam 1:12).

Fasting heightens our spiritual capacity to hear God's voice, intensifies our prayer, and leads us to be more conscious of obeying God (Is 58:6-9, Ezra 8:21-23; Dan 9:2-3, 21-22). It is a ministry unto God, gives Him glory (Acts 13:2) and shows our earnestness before God (Joel 2:12). It is also a self-discipline (1 Cor 9:27; 2 Pet 2:19; 1 Cor 6:12-13) that forces us to control the cravings and lusts of our physical body in order to raise our spiritual awareness and develop the fruit of the Spirit as a major part of our mature Christian life (Gal 5:22-23). It reveals the weaknesses of the flesh.

Fasting can also be warfare and shows our willingness to sacrifice to prevail and gain the victory, to break the yoke and set the captives free (Is 58:6).

Medical professionals agree that fasting is good for the body as it gives our system a chance to rid itself of toxins and fat and promotes heart health, blood sugar regulation, brain function, metabolism and cholesterol levels. A short fast is definitely healthy!

Lord Jesus, help me to control my body in order to raise my spiritual awareness.

Week 9, Day 3: Types of fasts

Then Ezra rose from before the house of God...he did not eat bread nor drink water, because he was mourning over the unfaithfulness of the exiles.
Ezra 10:6

There are different types of fasts, but most involve going without food. Fasting should be at the direction of the Lord and in consultation with your doctor. I have known two enthusiastic people who have ended up in hospital from fasting. The normal fast involves forgoing food but not water (2 Sam 12:16-22). This can be sustained by a healthy adult for up to 40 days, as Jesus did before He was launched into ministry (Matt 4:2-11). It is a time to seek God intensely. An absolute fast is the abstinence from both food and water (Acts 9:9, Ezra 10:6, Esther 4:16). This cannot be done for more than three days without supernatural intervention (Ex 34:28, Dt 9:9). This is generally used for desperate situations.

The Daniel fast (Dan 1:8-16, 10:3) is a preferable way to go for those with medical issues or for beginners, rather than attempting a long fast. Daniel chose a diet of vegetables and water (Dan 1:12) denying himself the king's choice food, meat and wine in order not to defile himself with food that was probably not kosher. This fast can be sustained for a considerable time if necessary. Alternatively, one could miss one or two meals a day to spend more time in prayer, but be careful not to overeat on the other meals!

There is also fasting from sleep in order to pray, which Jesus practised (Mk 1:35, Lk 6:12). Longer times of prayer are often held by groups in tandem, especially for regions or nations or in times of desperation.

How and when, Lord, would You have me fast?

Week 9, Day 4: How to fast

...when you fast, anoint your head and wash your face, so that your fasting will not be noticed by people, but by your Father who is in secret; and your Father who sees what is done in secret will reward you. Matthew 6:17-18

It is wise to prepare and start with a one-day fast then build up. Always ask the Lord and follow His instructions. If you are a heavy coffee or tea drinker, cut down beforehand or you can get nasty headaches as a withdrawal symptom. Fruit is the best way to lead into a fast. Do not precede a long fast with a big meal. This will exacerbate the hunger. The first 2-3 days are the worst for craving, hunger pangs and feeling faint or dizzy. After that you will feel increasingly strong and well up to between 21 and 40 days. Stop the fast if hunger pangs start at this stage, as the body is beginning to enter starvation and consume good tissue. Do not end a long fast with a huge meal. The body must be reawakened from hibernation, so begin with liquids like fruit juice, then gradually introduce solids and meat in small quantities.

Most of us eat far more than our body needs and obesity, greed and gluttony are widespread in Western culture. A little self-discipline will help to show us our weaknesses. A short temper, grumbling and becoming irritable arise quickly when we are hungry! However, if we push through, the fruit of the Spirit will begin to shine and we will be rewarded with hearing God better and find we receive breakthroughs in our prayers for the sacrifice we have made.

Dear Lord, make me willing to sacrifice to draw closer to You and become more effective in my prayer life.

Week 9, Day 5: The power of fasting

On exactly the tenth day of this seventh month is the Day of Atonement; it shall be a holy convocation for you, and you shall humble yourselves and present an offering by fire to the LORD. Leviticus 23:27

Israel is the only nation that is mandated by God to keep a national day of prayer and fasting. This is the Day of Atonement (Yom Kippur) which is still the most holy day in the Jewish calendar (Lev 16). It is a day to humble oneself, repent and get right with both God and one's fellow man. If Israel followed God's instructions, He promised to forgive their sin and the blood of the sacrificial animals would cover them – until Jesus became the perfect sacrifice.

In 1756 the King of England called the nation to prayer and fasting to invoke God's assistance in an invasion by France. God heard their cry and the country was saved. King George VI also called a day of prayer during WWII and the miracle of Dunkirk transpired.[1] In 1863, President Abraham Lincoln called Americans to a day of 'humiliation, fasting and prayer' during the Civil War, which was also effective.[2] God hears the cries of the humble.

Thank You Lord, that You hear the cries of your faithful people and You honour the sacrifice of fasting. I pray that leaders in our churches and government will know the power of prayer to change the course of history.

Week 9, Day 6: For such a time as this

Go, gather all the Jews who are found in Susa, and fast for me; do not eat or drink for three days, night or day. I and my attendants also will fast in the same way. And then I will go in to the king, which is not in accordance with the law; and if I perish, I perish. Esther 4:16

The Jewish people were facing annihilation at the hands of the wicked Haman who had tricked the king into issuing a deadly decree. A young queen was willing to put her life on the line to intercede for her people but requested that a total three-day fast be held on her behalf. There are times when drastic action is needed. As servants of the Lord, we need to recognise that prayer alone is not enough. When the disciples could not drive the epileptic demon out of the boy at the Mount of Transfiguration, Jesus said,

But this kind does not go out except by prayer and fasting. Matt 17:21 (NASB 1995)

If we are not seeing results from prayer, then a time of fasting may help us draw closer to God and bring the necessary breakthrough. God will honour that commitment. He still seeks those who will stand in the gap for their nation as Esther did, as it falls deeper into darkness and the inevitable judgements begin to play out.

'I searched for a man among them who would build up the wall and stand in the gap before Me for the land, so that I would not destroy it; but I found no one. Thus, I have poured out My indignation on them; I have consumed them with the fire of My wrath; their way I have brought upon their heads,' declares the Lord GOD. Ezek 22:30-31

Perhaps we are born for such a time as this to be the ones to avert disaster for our people.

Dear Lord Jesus, help me to be willing to sacrifice my time and my appetite to stand in the gap to see breakthroughs to my prayers for myself, my family, my church and my nation.

Week 9, Day 7: The chosen fast

Is this not the fast that I choose: To release the bonds of wickedness, to undo the ropes of the yoke, and to let the oppressed go free, and break every yoke? Is it not to break your bread with the hungry and bring the homeless poor into the house; when you see the naked, to cover him; and not to hide yourself from your own flesh? Isaiah 58:6-7

While fasting food is good, the chosen fast of the Lord is far more encompassing. It is basically doing what Jesus did in His ministry – to set the oppressed free and embrace and care for the needy and outcasts in society. He did not call the righteous but the sinners (Lk 5:32).

There are great rewards for those who repair the breach and glorify God by observing the Isaiah 58:5-12 fast. They shine forth His light and righteousness and can be assured that God will hear and answer their prayer (v.9). Physical restoration (v.8), guidance, provision, fulfilment and strength (v.11) are also rewards of this fast.

Father, You care so much for the poor. Show me the ones that I need to reach out to and show them your love. Make my heart willing to share what You have given me to provide for their needs.

Week 10
Thankfulness and prayer

Week 10, Day 1: Enter His courts

I will enter His gates with thanksgiving [Hebrew: toda] *and into His courts with praise* [tehillah] *and be thankful* [yada] *unto Him and bless* [baruch] *His name.* Psalm 100:4

A thankful heart will get us through the gates to where God is. It shows our appreciation for what God has given to us. When the Israelites grumbled about their leaders, God saw it as grumbling against Him (Ex 16:6-8). It caused a whole generation to lose their inheritance and die in the desert (Num 14:28-30). It destroys faith as it focuses on the problem, not the answer. How often do we murmur against our church leaders or governmental leaders instead of simply praying for them? I recommend *Grumble Fast* written by my friend Ruth Webb.[1]

It is easy to be thankful when things go well but quite another thing when the storms are raging against us. Christian maturity is learning to live in that place of praise and thanks as a lifestyle through thick and thin. This will separate us from the world as we stand in faith with a grateful heart. Thankfulness as a continual attitude of heart takes much effort to put into practice. Start by finding ten different things each day this week to thank God for.

You have turned my mourning into dancing for me; You have untied my sackcloth and encircled me with joy, that my soul may sing praise to You and not be silent. LORD my God, I will give thanks to You forever. Ps 30:11-12

Thank You, Lord for all your gracious gifts to me: for family, friends, sunshine and above all your presence. I will praise You while there is breath in my lungs.

Week 10, Day 2: In everything give thanks

...in everything give thanks; for this is God's will for you in Christ Jesus.
1 Thessalonians 5:18

We are asked to give thanks *in* everything, not *for* everything. Not everything that happens around us is praiseworthy. Some things are tragic and cause a huge amount of grief, like a car accident that obliterates a whole family. Our hearts will be much healthier if we focus on the positive even in bad circumstances and give thanks for any small joy we can find in the midst of pain.

One of the most beautiful books I have ever read is *One Thousand Gifts* by Ann Voskamp.[2] She was challenged to find 1,000 things to thank God for, and it changed her walk with God. She learnt to give thanks for all the little joys in the midst of raising six children with all the trials and tragedies of life, including her little sister being run over and killed by a truck on their own property when she was a child.

One year, when rehearsing for the Feast of Tabernacles in Jerusalem, we were staying out in the forest. While away, some of the rooms were raided by thieves from the neighbouring village. I remember watching in awe as one precious American lady went through her bag and thanked God for every item that was *not* taken. This is not a human reaction to such a circumstance.

Is there something today that you are finding it difficult to thank God for? In faith, praise Him that He has that situation in His mighty hand and will turn it for good. He is the God of the impossible.

Week 10, Day 3: God is faithful

The LORD's acts of mercy indeed do not end, for His compassions do not fail. They are new every morning; great is your faithfulness. Lamentations 3:22-23

Thankfulness is a choice. It is based on the fact that God is good and His faithfulness endures forever. Therefore, we can give thanks even when we don't feel like it. Our feelings should not dictate our faith. Our faith is based on who God is, not what we feel at any given time.

We thank God for what He has done; we praise Him for His character. The Hebrew way of saying 'Thank you' is to go and tell someone else what God (or someone else) has done. It is a *public* acknowledgement of His love or character with reference to God's name (Ex 15, 1 Chron 16:8-37). This is the meaning of praise, so the Old Testament words which are translated 'thanks' or 'thanksgiving' really mean 'praise' (usually *yada* and *toda*). Giving thanks is then a way of praising God.

If we endure, we will also reign with Him; If we deny Him, He will also deny us; if we are faithless, He remains faithful, for He cannot deny Himself. 2 Tim 2:12-13

Thankfully, God is faithful to His promises even when we are unfaithful to ours. We can therefore put our trust in Him and give Him thanks even when the clouds cover the sunshine and before we see the answer to our petition.

I remember how You have been faithful in the past and thank You today that You will always remain faithful. I thank You for all You have done previously and will do in the future.

Week 10, Day 4: The sacrifice of thanksgiving

Those who sacrifice thank-offerings honour me, and to the blameless I will show my salvation. Psalm 50:23 (NIVUK)

The thank offering was one kind of peace offering (Lev 7:11-18; Ps 107:21-22; Ps 116:17), as were the vow and freewill offerings. These were not obligatory, but showed a desire for closer fellowship with God. A sacrifice of thanksgiving is a ministry to God, rather than to others. We can never outgive God, as He will always bless us more abundantly than we can give (Mal 3:10; 2 Cor 9:6; Acts 20:35; 2 Sam 24:24).

Although a blood sacrifice is no longer needed since God has sacrificed His Son for us, the principle of sacrifice still remains. It is the character of love to want to give to the one you love – ask any parent! Our offering is now a thankful heart that praises God's character and is grateful for His daily mercies. It finds the good in the difficult times and brings peace and confidence in God. This uplifts not only ourselves but others around us too.

Through Him then, let us continually offer up a sacrifice of praise to God, that is, the fruit of lips that give thanks to His name. Heb 13:15

Dear Lord, I desire to offer to You this day a sacrifice of praise that will be a sweet aroma before the throne of God. Let me rise above my feelings and come into your gates with thanksgiving in my heart.

Week 10, Day 5: First fruits

When you enter the land which I am going to give to you and you gather its harvest, then you shall bring in the sheaf of the first fruits of your harvest to the priest. Leviticus 23:10

The First Fruits festival was to be a time of joy and celebration. The sheaf of grain or basket of fruit was offered to the Lord in thankfulness for the harvest that was to come. But the principle of offering the first to God applies much more broadly than just food or goods. Humanity's first day on earth after creation was to be a Sabbath to spend with the Lord as a first fruit of time. The day began in the temple at dawn with a thanksgiving service. The first of the month was to be remembered. When planting fruit trees, it was forbidden to eat the fruit for the first three years, then the fourth year was to be offered to the Lord and only in the fifth year could the fruit be eaten (Lev 19:23-25). The first-born of animals were to be sacrificed to God and the first-born son of the family was to be redeemed with a sacrifice as they were holy to God (Ex 13:11-15).

Jesus was raised from the dead on the festival of First Fruits in fulfilment of this prophetic feast.

But the fact is, Christ has been raised from the dead, the first fruits of those who are asleep. 1 Cor 15:20

We now have confidence that we too will be raised from the dead to live with Him. Offering the first fruits to God is an act of faith that the abundance and fullness is coming and an offering of thankfulness to God for His goodness.

Thank You, Lord that your resurrection, as the first fruit, assures us of eternal life. Jn 3:16

Week 10, Day 6: Finding the good in the bad

And we know that God causes all things to work together for good to those who love God, to those who are called according to His purpose. Romans 8:28

We are God's children and our Father works all things together for good if we love Him. Many people feel they are being hypocritical if they thank God for what appears bad. Hypocrisy is refusing to practise what you believe; it does not mean refusing to practise what you feel. What we believe is shown by what we do, not what we say. If we live by faith and not by feelings we will enter God's realm of reality. The reality of the spiritual realm is greater than what we see with our physical eyes.

Nick Vujicic was born with no arms or legs and a tiny foot. Today he would most likely be aborted before even seeing the light of day. Yet he has inspired millions as a motivational speaker and evangelist. What the world sees as a worthless life, God sees as precious, and He can redeem and restore broken pieces. I love the Japanese art of kintsugi. This art form uses gold to piece together broken shards of pottery or glass to make something more beautiful than the original object. That is what God does!

It is awesome to see how God can bring a positive outcome out of dreadful circumstances if we will just offer them to Him in confidence and faith. Sometimes it is necessary to have the seed fall into the ground before we see the fruit of our labours (Jn 12:24).

Father, help me this day to rise up into your reality. I offer You my broken pieces and ask You to add your gold in the cracks to repair and create something beautiful in my life. Thank You.

Week 10, Day 7: The privilege of thanksgiving

Whenever the living creatures give glory, honour and thanks to him who sits on the throne and who lives for ever and ever, the twenty-four elders fall down before him who sits on the throne and worship him who lives for ever and ever... Revelation 4:9-10b (NIVUK)

The book of Revelation especially gives us some peeks into what is happening in heaven. We see thanks, praise and worship being continually offered before the throne of God. Thanksgiving is happening directly in God's presence. It is a privilege we have, to give Him praise, knowing that He desires to inhabit our praise (Ps 22:3).

We are exhorted over forty times in the Psalms alone to give thanks to God. It gives Him pleasure. As the spirit of this world wants us to focus on ourselves and our own pleasure, not what pleases God, ingratitude is a sign of the end times (2 Tim 3:2). Gratitude sets us immediately apart and is a hallmark of maturity. Our 'inner health' becomes audible when we are thankful. If we are insecure, we will not be able to praise God or others or build others up, as we are still craving to be built up ourselves.

When we can sail our ship steadfastly though the rough seas and react calmly to difficult circumstances, people begin to sit up and listen and ask questions. We develop this ability to rise above the circumstances by our faith and keeping our eyes on Jesus. God is the measure of reality, not the world around us. He is in charge and so we can trust Him and thank Him.

Dear Lord, help me to cling to You even through turbulent waters and know that You are the one who calms the storms and takes me by the hand to walk over the billowing waves.

The Many Facets of Prayer

Week 11
Praise and prayer

Week 11, Day 1: Hallelujah

Praise the LORD [Hebrew: hallelujah], *all nations; laud Him* [shabchu], *all peoples! For His lovingkindness is great toward us, and the truth of the* LORD *is everlasting. Praise the* LORD*!* [hallelujah] Psalm 117:1-2 (NASB1995)

Learning to praise the Lord is an essential facet of prayer. If you know one Hebrew word it may well be *hallelujah*. *Hallel* is used over eighty times in the Psalms, often as a command. It has meanings of boasting, lauding, glorifying a superior object or person for its or their superior qualities; being foolishly in love or abandoning self.

The Psalms are full of praise and are a wonderful source of learning how to praise God. He is so great that there is much for which we can praise Him. The Levitical musicians were commissioned to give thanks and praise in the temple daily. In the services, He is praised for His loving kindness, His faithfulness and for all His goodness to Israel.

Music is so readily available these days over the internet, one does not have to be a musician to access songs of worship and praise. Music helps us to remember the words, and it was the major means used for praise in the temple. David was a harpist and he wrote many of the psalms. Asaph and other Levites also wrote psalms. But, it is not essential to use music; you can just use your voice to shout praise to God.

God can be praised by various means, but essentially the Lord must be recognised, affirmed and verbally acknowledged with joy aloud (Ps 84:4, 102:18, 113:3). Though it is always good to be thankful, focus your praise on God's character and works, not on what He has done for you personally, to keep the focus on Him not on 'me'.

Praise the Lord aloud today with joy, for He is worthy of our praise.

Week 11, Day 2: Telling others

I will give thanks [odeh] to the Lord with all my heart; I will tell of all your wonders. I will be glad and exult in You; I will sing praise [azmerah] to Your name, O Most High. Psalm 9:1-2 (NASB1995)

It may seem strange, but the word *odeh* is related to the root *yada*, a very common word for praise, but often translated as thanks. It can mean to confess sin or to confess God's character or works, or the character of a person. It is making a public proclamation of God's attributes – who He is and what He does. In modern Hebrew, *yad* means hand and also can be an organisation that lends a helping hand. In two forms of yada it means to 'throw' or 'cast'.

Lift up your hands to the sanctuary and bless the LORD. Ps 134:2

We can raise our hands to heaven, clap our hands, or stretch out our hands to receive what God has for us. We can also pass that blessing on to others and tell them it is a gift from God who loves them. Some examples are Gen 29:35, 2 Chron 20:21, Ps 107:15 and Ps 139:14.

Lord, show me who I can tell about your goodness today. I stretch out my hands before You to praise You and also to receive with open hands what You would care to give to me today.

Week 11, Day 3: Bless

Bless [barchi] *the Lord, O my soul! O Lord my God, You are very great; You are clothed with splendour and majesty.* Psalm 104:1

The word 'bless' in regards to praise is related to blessing God. How do we bless someone who is all-sufficient? God does not need anything from us, and we cannot give Him anything that He does not already have. But He created us out of His love because He wants relationship with us. Therefore, the first thing we can bless Him with is our time, since it takes time to develop relationship. We can give Him our heart, our love and our earthly resources, which He will then multiply. Where we spend our time, money and energy displays where our heart really lies. If we have priorities other than God's purposes, we need to reorganise our life to put His Kingdom first. We can bless Him by our prayers and by joining Him in His work and make Him known to the world to establish His Kingdom on earth as it is in heaven.

King David made many mistakes – grave ones, including adultery, murder and pride – that cost thousands of lives, but his heart was humble and right before God. God forgave his sins and restored him. The Messiah, Jesus, is from his generational line. He blessed the Lord by pouring out his heart in poetry and songs of thanksgiving, praise and worship, remembering God's goodness and mercy. His legacy remains to this day. Read Job 1:21, Ps 96:2 and 1 Chron 29:10.

Try writing a psalm that will bless the Lord today.

Week 11, Day 4: Praise God inhabits

Yet you are holy, You who are enthroned upon the praises of Israel. Psalm 22:3

What a beautiful picture. God delights in this deep-seated praise. Psalm 22 is a cry from the heart when David felt forsaken by God, and it was quoted by Jesus on the cross. This is the hardest time to praise God. Yet if we can rise above our emotions and trust and praise God, it gives Him great pleasure. This *tehillah* praise is the praise that acknowledges God's sovereignty in all circumstances and sees Him seated above our problems, enthroned in the heavenlies above all powers and principalities operating in the world. If we focus on Jesus and sing to Him, it will change us and lift us out of the miry clay.

To grant those who mourn in Zion, giving them a garland instead of ashes, the oil of gladness instead of mourning, the cloak of praise instead of a disheartened spirit... Is 61:3

It is the garment of praise that the Lord gives us when we are in despair. This high praise is extremely powerful to dispel the enemy's efforts to discourage us.

The high praises of God shall be in their mouths, and a two-edged sword in their hands, to execute vengeance on the nations, and punishment on the peoples, to bind their kings with chains, and their dignitaries with shackles of iron, to execute against them the judgment written... Ps 149:6-9a

His presence descends in a cloud of glory and He 'inhabits' our praises. Some other references are Ps 147:1, Dt 10:21, 1 Chron 16:35, Neh 9:5 and Ex 15:11.

Dear Lord, take me to this place of praise where the enemy cannot touch me, where I am sheltered in the rock with You and I can praise You above all earthly circumstances.

Week 11, Day 5: Singing and music

I will praise [ahalah] *the Lord while I live; I will sing praises* [azemrah] *to my God while I have my being.* Psalm 146:2

Zamar is a poetic term used almost exclusively in the Psalms. It means to make music with our voices or with instruments. David established 24-hour worship in the tabernacle to be a joyful sound to the Lord. Psalm 150 lists trumpets, harps, lyres, timbrels, cymbals, stringed and wind instruments. As well as instruments, there was a Levitical choir in the temple for daily services. At the dedication of the temple in 2 Chron 5:11-14 and its rededication in Nehemiah 12:27-47, and at the major pilgrimage feasts, there were great musical celebrations.

Praise music can be loud but should not be deafening. Our music should always be bringing people closer to God, not driving them away by excessive volume or whipping them up into an orgy-like frenzy. The enemy wants to capture our sensual side, as we see by the use of music, especially drumming, in pagan and satanic festivals.

The arts are created to glorify our Maker. Many psalms speak about singing a 'new song' (Ps 33:3, 40:3, 96:1, 98:1, 144:9, 149:1). God delights in our creativity being expressed and used for His glory. There are still new songs being written in heaven (Rev 5:9, 14:3).

If you are musical, ask Him for a new song. You can always sing a few verses of the Psalms and see what God will give you. Ps 28:7, 81:2, 104:33, 149:3, 1 Chron 16:9, Ex 15:2

Week 11, Day 6: Shout

One generation shall praise [yeshabach] *Your works to another, and shall declare Your mighty acts.* Psalm 145:4

Shabach means to laud or praise in a loud voice or to shout. Our shout is powerful in the heavenlies. It echoes through the generations in the verse above. It is a shout of joy that comes from a righteous heart and praises the King of kings.

Be glad in the LORD and rejoice, you righteous ones; and shout for joy, all you who are upright in heart. Ps 32:11

It is the type of praise that Daniel offered to God when He revealed the king's dream to him (Dan 2:23) and also was given by Nebuchadnezzar when he recognised the true God (Dan 4:34).

We shout for our favourite football team or sports stars, but how many of us have welcomed the heavenly King with a shout? After all, He is far more worthy to receive our praise (Ps 63:3, Ps 147:12).

Oh Lord, You are so worthy. Forgive me that I am more inclined to shout praise to an earthly star than to You. Take me to high praise that will erupt into a shout of praise that will rise to your throne room and welcome You.

Week 11, Day 7: Physical praise

They shall praise His name with dancing; they shall sing praises to Him with tambourine and lyre. Psalm 149:3

These words – dance (Ps 30:11), rejoice, exalt, clap (Ps 47:1), kneel, give (Ps 96:8) – and others are often used interchangeably in poetic Hebrew parallelism. They are all forms of doing one thing – honouring and praising God.

You may be thinking, *but I'm not a loud, extroverted person*. Well, that's okay – silence and reverence are also ways of honouring God (Ps 46:10). But in the end, it is not a matter of how we are comfortable, but how God wants to be honoured and praised. If the Scripture says that this is what brings Him pleasure, then we need to rise above our inhibitions and do what He enjoys.

In some Christian circles, especially more traditional denominations, prayer is more a silent or quiet pursuit between you and God alone, but as we have seen, praise is much more about publicly declaring and proclaiming God's character and works. Praise gives glory to God. When we praise God as part of our prayer, our prayers definitely should not be hushed and quiet. They can be expressed aloud verbally and physically through kneeling or dancing or singing, whether we are alone or in groups.

Lord God, teach me to express my praise to You with my body, not just my mind and lips. Help me experiment with new ways of creativity that will give You glory.

The Many Facets of Prayer

Week 12
Worship and prayer

Week 12, Day 1: Praise or worship?

How lovely are Your dwelling places, O LORD of hosts! My soul longed and even yearned for the courts of the LORD; My heart and my flesh sing for joy to the living God. Psalm 84:1-2 (NASB1995)

A worshipper is one who loves to be in God's company and dwell in His courts. We enter with thanksgiving and praise but worship is where we abide with the Lord in the inner sanctum in His presence. We could perhaps say that praise is like dating but worship is like marriage. Praise can require faith and involves the body, the mind and the will. Worship is a matter of the heart moved by a desire for intimacy with the Lord. To truly worship, we are motivated by love not duty and pre-occupied with who God is and being immersed in Him. It is a place of rest in the Father's arms. It is the response to the presence of God which has manifested as a result of our praise. Whereas praise is verbal, worship is often more quiet and gentle. Praise can involve warfare as in Psalm 149, but when we are in worship, the angels are doing the warfare for us!

Joshua had a worshipper's heart (Ex 33:11) and so did Anna in the New Testament (Lk 2:36-38). The psalmist of Psalm 84 did also. All just wanted to linger in God's presence.

For a day in Your courts is better than a thousand outside. I would rather stand at the threshold of the house of my God than dwell in the tents of wickedness. Ps 84:10

A real worshipper is willing to tarry with the Lord rather than just finish the obligatory service.

Dear Lord, please give me the heart of a worshipper – to love being with You and just enjoy your presence.

Week 12, Day 2: The secret place

*One thing I have asked from the L*ORD*, that I shall seek: that I may dwell in the house of the L*ORD *all the days of my life, to behold the beauty of the L*ORD *and to meditate in His temple. For in the day of trouble He will conceal me in His tabernacle; in the secret place of His tent He will hide me; He will lift me up on a rock…When You said, 'Seek My face,' my heart said to You, "Your face, O L*ORD*, I shall seek."* Psalm 27:4-5, 8 (NASB1995)

David was another worshipper who loved to meditate on the Lord and to seek His face. He knew that in God's presence was a safe place where trouble could not overcome him. It is a place of strength. This is a far cry from telling God what we want Him to do for us or ticking off the boxes on a prayer list. This is deep communication and intimate relationship. We don't just hop into this place. Our times of prayer will flow from thanksgiving to praise, then into worship. In this intimate place, we hear from God and begin to see things from His perspective. Our desires meld into His and we can see what is on heaven's agenda and join with the intercession of Jesus. This is far more exciting than just lifting up names and issues before God.

Worship is what we were created to do. It is all that we are, responding to all that He is. As William Temple said, 'To worship is to quicken the conscience by the holiness of God, to feed the mind with the truth of God, to purge the imagination by the beauty of God, to open the heart to the love of God, and to devote the will to the purpose of God.'[1]

Heavenly Father, take me deeper into this secret place with You this day.

Week 12, Day 3: Bowing down

Come, let us worship [shachah] *and bow down, let us kneel before the LORD our Maker.* Psalm 95:6

The Hebrew word *shachah* means to bow down and prostrate oneself in worship, to be humbled or brought low (Josh 5:14). It is the old image of bowing down before a king to pay homage. We still see this in the Muslim world where they prostrate themselves before Allah.

Bowing down implies accepting an entity as being superior or more worthy of adoration than oneself. It requires humility and change. It was pride that caused Satan to fall (Ezek 28:11-19, Is 14:12-17) and pride that causes most people to reject God. We like to be our own master rather than handing over that lordship to Jesus.

...for you shall not worship [shachah] *any other god, for the LORD, whose name is Jealous, is a jealous God.* Ex 34:14

The first commandment forbids us to make or bow down to any image or any other god except Yahweh (Ex 20:3-6). In the Sermon on the Mount, Jesus peeled the action of the law back to the motives of the heart (Matt 5). Humility is an essential element of worship.

Heavenly Father, I humble my heart today that I may truly worship You with all my being. Show me where I am still resisting You and not allowing You full reign.

Week 12, Day 4: In Spirit and truth

Yet a time is coming and has now come when the true worshippers will worship the Father in the Spirit and in truth, for they are the kind of worshippers the Father seeks. God is spirit, and his worshippers must worship in the Spirit and in truth. John 4:23-24 (NIVUK)

The Father is seeking worshippers who will fulfil this desire of His heart. When Esther was summoned to go before the king, she could choose anything to take with her (Esther 2:13); however, she knew it was not her choice that mattered. She consulted the king's eunuch and took only what he recommended (v.15). To gain the king's favour, his choice was paramount.

The Greek word for worship, *proskuneo,* is similar to the Hebrew, meaning to bow down or pay homage to a deity, prostrate oneself, serve, kiss (as a dog licks his master's hand).

As the owner of a small dog, I understand the loving lick from my little companion! My previous border collie would lie on the floor with chin on the front paws as I ate breakfast, watching my every move for any sign that the morning walk was about to take place. That is how we should be with our heavenly Master: with eyes on Him, available at His beck and call.

God's *ecclesia*, His bride, is preparing herself for the wedding, worshipping in Spirit and truth. It is the presence of the Holy Spirit that makes worship possible. He helps us to pray and worship, perfects what we offer and makes it effective. Spirit-led worship overflows into a Spirit-led life and Spirit-empowered service.

Dear Lord, You sent your Spirit to lead me into truth and enable me to worship the Father spirit to Spirit. Have your way in me today.

Week 12, Day 5: Reverence

But the Lord answered and said to her, 'Martha, Martha, you are worried and distracted by many things; but only one thing is necessary; for Mary has chosen the good part, which shall not be taken away from her.' Luke 10:41-42

Martha was busy preparing dinner for the guests while Mary was sitting at Jesus' feet, preoccupied with His presence and listening to Him. Ecclesiastes teaches us that there is a time for everything under the sun (Ecc 3:1-8). When Jesus is in the house, it is a time to stop all else and listen. Other things will fall into place when we put Him first, rather than being busy doing all that the world demands of us. It is a time to 'be', not to 'do'. False gods always want us to do works to gain their approval and earn our salvation. We can never earn our salvation. That is why we need the Saviour and why Jesus had to die on the cross to take our place to save us.

Mary chose the better way. She was face to face with Jesus in reverence, awe and devotion. She had been forgiven much and she loved deeply. While there are many ways that we can praise God, worship is simply an intimate relationship of awe and wonder, sitting at Jesus' feet (Acts 18:7,13; 19:27; Mk 7:7). It is loving God, not through doing, just by being.

Take time today to sit at Jesus' feet in awe and adoration.

Week 12, Day 6: Bond-servant

Therefore, I urge you, brethren, by the mercies of God, to present your bodies a living and holy sacrifice, acceptable to God, which is your spiritual service of worship [latreia]. Romans 12:1 (NASB1995)

There is an element in both Hebrew and Greek *(latreuo)* where the word worship means service, especially the service of ministry in the temple (both the sacrifices and musical offerings) and the ministry of intercession between mankind and God.

It is God's desire to have a kingdom of priests who will know Him face to face (Ex 19:6, 1 Pet 2:9). The priests were called to holiness and this is reflected in the verse above in the New Testament, now applied to the priesthood of all believers. The priests were set apart from other duties to work for God alone. It is not service for the sake of duty – it is to be a holy service of dedication to the Lord. When the priesthood became corrupt, the nation went likewise. If Satan can infiltrate the church leadership, he can take the whole church, and as the church should be guiding the nation morally, if we renege on speaking and living the truth, then the nation will fall also.

Paul and the other apostles saw themselves as a bond-servants to the Lord (Rom 1:1, Phil 1:1, Jas 1:1, 2 Pet 1:1, Jude 1:1, Lk 1:38). A bond-servant was a slave who voluntarily chose to remain with their master when they could have gone free (Ex 21:1-6). They had no rights but they were provided for. Jesus also took the form of a bond-servant.

Have this attitude in yourselves which was also in Christ Jesus, who, as He already existed in the form of God, did not consider equality with God something to be grasped, but emptied Himself by taking the form of a bond-servant and being born in the likeness of men. Phil 2:5-7

Father, I choose to be a bond-servant for You today. Help me to lay down all my 'rights' and accept the cross You choose to give me to shape my character and make me into your image.

Week 12, Day 7: Heavenly worship

All the angels were standing round the throne and round the elders and the four living creatures. They fell down on their faces before the throne and worshipped God, saying: 'Amen! Praise and glory and wisdom and thanks and honour and power and strength be to our God for ever and ever. Amen!' Revelation 7:11-12 (NIVUK)

When we read the book of Revelation and catch a glimpse of the worship of heaven, we see that it is entirely focussed on the Lord. Words like holy, worthy, majesty, glory, power, blessing, honour, dominion and thanks are declared. There is no pleading with God; just acknowledgement of His attributes.

Worship comes before work. All ministry to people must flow out from our ministering to the Lord. Otherwise, we act in our strength and without faith it is impossible to please Him (Heb 11:6). When we worship, God reveals Himself and we become like Him. From this we naturally do what He wants. If we allow His life to flow through us then we'll never suffer burnout. Worship is a place of rest, not work.

Consequently, there remains a Sabbath rest for the people of God. For the one who has entered His rest has himself also rested from his works, as God did from His. Heb 4:9-10

The Lord wants us to rest in Him. God created the Sabbath for us to enjoy Him and to rest from our labours. Worship is that place. When our prayer flows from worship then it will accomplish much, as it is God-conceived and God-initiated. Prayer then becomes a creative agent to bring change in any situation.

Rest in the arms of the Lord today. Lay all burdens at His feet and receive His perspective.

Week 13

The prayers of Jesus

Week 13, Day 1: Jesus' life of prayer

But the news about Him was spreading even farther, and large crowds were gathering to hear Him and to be healed of their sicknesses. But Jesus Himself would often slip away to the wilderness and pray. Luke 5:15-16

Jesus' life was embedded in prayer. He had a constant connection with His Father that stemmed from seeing what the Father wanted to do and doing it (Jn 8:28-29). He did nothing on His own initiative. We are not given a lot of details of His prayers, but it is recorded that He often went to a private, quiet place to pray (Mk 1:35 – early morning secluded place, Lk 5:16 – regular occurrence, Lk 9:18 – praying alone, Lk 11:1 – before teaching to pray, Lk 6:12 – whole night in prayer before choosing the 12 disciples). He prayed at other events such as His baptism (Lk 3:21), the transfiguration (Lk 9:28-29) and ascension (Lk 24:50-51) and before healing the deaf-mute (Mk 7:34).

He also had a life of thanksgiving (Matt 11:25-26, Jn 11:41-42) and was in the Jewish habit of blessing the Father before meals as seen at Emmaus (Lk 24:30-31) and the Passover meal (Lk 22:17-19) as well as before feeding the 5,000 (Matt 14:19) and the 4,000 (Mk 8:6).

In the garden (John 12:27-28), we see Jesus in agonising prayer as He strengthened Himself for the horrific sacrifice He was about to endure. He prayed for Peter (Lk 22:31-32) and even on the cross He was still praying (Lk 23:34, Matt 27:46, Lk 23:46, Heb 5:7-8).

Dear Lord, please teach me to emulate your constant walk of prayer and abide in You and You in me. Open my eyes to see what the Father is wanting to do and be obedient to do it.

Week 13, Day 2: Praying for children

Then some children were brought to Him so that He would lay His hands on them and pray; and the disciples rebuked them. Matthew 19:13

It is touching to see how Jesus cared for the little children and gave us an example from them of how we should approach the Father. It is still a Jewish tradition, as part of the Sabbath prayers each Friday night before the meal, for the father of the household to lay hands on the heads of each of his children and pray for them, as well as to bless his wife. Many Jews say that the Sabbath has kept them rather than them keeping the Sabbath. It has certainly helped to keep even non-religious Jewish families together.

It is powerful to pray blessing over our children. It releases them to God, imparts God's best into their lives and assures them that both we and God are on their side. Let us learn from their simple faith and trust and come to our heavenly Father the same way, accepting His embrace.

'Truly I say to you, whoever does not receive the kingdom of God like a child will not enter it at all.' And He took them in His arms and began blessing them, laying His hands on them. Mk 10:15-16

Heavenly Father, You are the source of all blessing. I pray blessing over my children, grandchildren, and all the children You bring to my mind this morning.

Week 13, Day 3: Our Father

Our Father who is in heaven, hallowed be Your name. Your kingdom come, Your will be done, on earth as it is in heaven. Matthew 6:9-10

When Jesus was asked by His disciples to teach them to pray, He told them not to make meaningless repetitions as the Gentiles do. Most Jews only pray from a prayer book or set prayers written by the rabbis. Jesus did not give the disciples a lengthy prayer to keep repeating. He gave a succinct model or pattern of prayer.

The first part of the prayer is addressing the Father, Abba, Daddy. We are blessed that we can enter His presence and know that our prayers reach the throne room in heaven. He then recognised the holiness of God and the supremacy of His name. The message that Jesus preached was the gospel of the Kingdom of God – His righteous reign over all the earth. This Kingdom already reigns in the heavens and it is for us to join the task to bring this Kingdom to earth – for God's will to be done on the earth as in heaven. Heaven is to invade earth through us, in the church and in the world. Are we actively praying for that?

Thank You, Abba for your Father's heart that protects, provides and loves us.

I thank You, Jesus, that your name is above every other name and that every knee will bow and tongue confess that You are Lord. Let your Kingdom invade my life and your will be done through me today.

Week 13, Day 4: Give us this day

Give us this day our daily bread. And forgive us our debts, as we also have forgiven our debtors. And do not lead us into temptation, but deliver us from evil. For Yours is the kingdom and the power and the glory forever. Amen. Matthew 6:11-13

The second part of Jesus' prayer focusses on our need. He asks the Father for our daily provision, not for the distant future. Jesus said each day has enough worries of its own (Matt 6:31-34) and the Father will provide for us just as He does for the birds.

Next, He reminds us of our need for forgiveness and that we must forgive others in order to receive God's forgiveness. The greatest debt we have is that we are sinners and the wages of sin is death. Jesus paid this huge cost for us with His life so we can be free and blessed.

Temptation is all around us and within us, especially now with the web making advertising and accessibility so easy. As Jesus prayed for Peter not to fall into temptation, so He prays for us (Lk 22:31-32). We live in a world where evil abounds, but we must keep our eyes fixed on Jesus and not let the things of the world discourage or distract us from God's Kingdom purposes. We are to be the light in the darkness and force the darkness to flee rather than allowing it to consume us (Is 9:2).

Jesus finished the prayer by looking to heaven and reminding us that the Father is all powerful and His Kingdom will prevail. All glory to God!

Thank You, Father, that You will provide all my needs this day. I choose to forgive all those who have hurt me. Let me not fall into temptation or any traps of the enemy. May You be glorified in my life today and your Kingdom and power be demonstrated through me. Amen

Week 13, Day 5: The high priestly prayer

I am not asking on behalf of these alone, but also for those who believe in Me through their word, that they may all be one, just as You, Father, are in Me, and I in You, that they also may be in Us, so that the world may believe that You sent Me. John 17:20-21

John chapter 17 is the longest of Jesus' prayers that is recorded. Over three years of ministry, He had glorified God by making the Father known through word and deed. His disciples now understood He was the Messiah and after they received the Holy Spirit, they would continue His work on earth as He returned to heaven. He had accomplished the work that the Father had set for Him.

Firstly, Jesus prayed that God would keep, guard and protect the disciples from the evil one and that they would be one as He and the Father are one. He asked that they would have joy and be made holy through the Word of truth, so that the world would believe in Jesus. He also prayed that through God's glory and abiding in Jesus, their unity would be perfected and God's love spread abroad. He prayed for them to see God's glory and be with Him where He was. He promised to keep making His name known to the disciples so they would know the love of God living in them.

The greatest weapon of Satan is to sow disunity in the body of Christ, as it is in unity and love that God reveals His name and compassion to the world. As weak human beings, we need the love of God and power of the Holy Spirit to bring the unity we cannot obtain in our own strength. This is Jesus' greatest wish and brings God glory. Where unity prevails, it has power to bring revival and great breakthrough in prayer.

Dear Father, release this unity in our families, churches and regions. Break every stronghold that causes disunity and fill the cracks with your love from heaven.

Week 13, Day 6: Gethsemane

He knelt down and began to pray, saying, 'Father, if You are willing, remove this cup from Me; yet not My will, but Yours be done.' [Now an angel from heaven appeared to Him, strengthening Him. And being in agony He was praying very fervently; and His sweat became like drops of blood, falling down upon the ground]. Luke 22:41b-44

Jesus' most fervent prayer was at Gethsemane. In fact, He prayed it three times. Sometimes we have to battle through our desires when we know what God is saying, as our flesh is weak, even when the spirit is willing. There is always a cost to discipleship. We have to bear a cross and it is the same one of sacrifice that Jesus bore, but not, thankfully, to the same extent. The flesh must die for the spirit to live. The cost may be in losing our family for walking in righteousness, losing our reputation, our job, our financial security, even our life for the sake of the gospel. Be assured, Jesus is praying for us in this battle and He has angels at His disposal.

At these crossroads, we can turn away, but that is an even bigger price to pay than the price to follow Jesus at all cost. Jesus will always be there when we accept His call. All that we need will be provided, even when we cannot see how. Expect miracles. God will be glorified as we walk in faith and take a leap of faith, hanging on to God alone.

Dear Lord Jesus, You did not shun the agony of the cross for my sake. Help me never to be ashamed of You and always to obey your voice when You call me.

Week 13, Day 7: Prayers from the cross

And about the ninth hour Jesus cried out with a loud voice, saying, 'Eli, Eli lema sabaktanei?' that is, 'My God, my God, why have You forsaken me?' Matthew 27:46

Sometimes we feel that God has abandoned us, but of course, He hasn't, as He has promised never to leave us nor forsake us (Dt 3:8, Heb 13:5). However, He did momentarily turn His face away from Jesus on the cross as He paid the price for sin which separates us from God. Jesus became the curse for us in that moment to redeem us from the curse (Dt 21:23, Gal 3:13-14). Psalm 22:1-2 has been fulfilled. With God, we can now overcome hopelessness by the blood of the Lamb and despair has to go, as the presence of God is with us.

But Jesus was saying, 'Father, forgive them; for they do not know what they are doing.' Lk 23:34

If you feel God has vanished, then check that you have forgiven everyone and have done the last thing He told you to do. Even on the cross, Jesus was forgiving those who were causing Him such agony. Unforgiveness will block the presence of God. In the end, we may just need to walk by faith and not by feelings. The sun still shines, even when clouds are blocking its light and warmth. We believe the Word is true and sooner or later the Son will break through.

And Jesus, crying out with a loud voice, said, 'Father, into Your Hands I entrust my Spirit.' And having said this, He died. Lk 23:46

Our trust in God will take us to be where Jesus is in glory. We have the assurance of eternal life because He has gone before us to prepare the way and given us this wonderful promise (Jn 3:16).

Thank You, Father, that You never leave me. My hope and trust are in You even when I do not feel it. I bless You for who You are and that You have all things in your control.

Week 14
Praying the Psalms

Week 14, Day 1: Sweet psalmist

David the son of Jesse declares, the man who was raised on high, the anointed of the God of Jacob, and the sweet psalmist of Israel. 2 Samuel 23:1

David was the youngest of eight sons of Jesse. He was a gifted musician (1 Sam 16:18) who seemed to learn and perfect his art in the fields as he was caring for sheep. That meant that he started by singing and playing to God alone. But such was his talent and anointing that he was brought into the royal courts of Saul to calm his soul when he was tormented by evil spirits (1 Sam 16:23). Anointed music sets an atmosphere of worship, and demons cannot stay where worship resides.

David was anointed probably as a teenager. His family did not even call him in to see the prophet until Samuel had rejected all his brothers. It was over a decade until he became king at age 30 (2 Sam 5:4). Perhaps you also are in a time of waiting to be released into your full destiny. You know you have been called by God, but it seems that no door has opened as yet. God used the interim difficult years to prepare David's heart to rule in righteousness. Do not despise the years of preparation God may be putting you through, and do not give up. God may have more for you than you can even ask for or conceive, and it will be worth it in the end. Follow the Lord faithfully in the small things and He can catapult you to much larger responsibilities if you have, like David, withstood the times of being pursued by a jealous, power-seeking person, or like Joseph, spent years in prison under false allegations.

Father, keep me faithful during times of trouble and teach me to walk in your ways with a pure heart.

Week 14, Day 2: A man after God's own heart

...He raised up David to be their king, concerning whom He also testified and said, 'I have found David, the son of Jesse, a man after My heart, who will do all My will.' Acts 13:22

David's life of worship was so impacting that his psalms have formed almost half the book of Psalms. The term *l'David,* meaning to, for or by David, heads 73 psalms, thirteen of which refer to incidents in David's life (Ps 3, 7, 18, 34, 51, 52, 54, 56, 57, 59, 60, 63, 142).

David was not the people's choice for a king, but God chose him because he was a man after God's own heart (1 Sam 13:14). He had a deep relationship with God and became a forerunner for the Messianic King to come. Eighteen of his psalms appear to be written in times of trouble, several while he was fleeing from Saul and living in caves in the desert (e.g. Ps 18, 52, 54, 59). His danger was very physical and very real. He poured out his heart, but he never ended in despair. He trusted in the Lord to deliver him (Ps 52, 61, 62, 131, 143). That is a great lesson for us to keep our focus on Him in hard times and not dwell on the problems. Perhaps we are also not ones the world would choose, but God can use any willing heart.

Lord, may I be known as a person who has a heart after You and does your will. Find a psalm today that you can memorize and use in times of despair or danger.

Week 14, Day 3: Psalms of praise and thanksgiving

LORD, our Lord, how majestic is your name in all the earth, You who have displayed Your splendour above the heavens! Psalm 8:1

Psalms of praise are plentiful and were used in the temple worship. The praise is always directed towards God for His character and His acts, especially the Lord's actions in Israel's history or creation (e.g. Ps 8, 29, 33, 104, 111, 113 etc.). Most were meant for general worship but some were used for particular festivals. They were probably mostly used for corporate rather than individual worship. Songs of thanksgiving (e.g. Ps 4, 9, 16, 34, 124, 138), on the other hand, were probably most often sung by individuals but may have been used corporately. For example, they could have been sung formally in conjunction with a thank offering for a blessing received. Such a celebration was normally shared with family or friends.

Your vows are binding upon me, God; I will render thanksgiving offerings to You. For You have saved my soul from death, indeed my feet from stumbling, so that I may walk before God in the light of the living. Ps 56:12-13

Following this tradition, the psalms of praise and thanksgiving are widely read or sung in the synagogue services and this is replicated in many church denominations, especially the more traditional ones. The first sermon on Australian soil by Rev. Richard Johnson on February 3, 1788, was from Psalm 116:12-13, giving thanks to the Lord for the safe arrival of the First Fleet. It is good to read a psalm of praise or thanksgiving on waking to focus our thoughts on God (Ps 100:4).

Give the Lord a thank offering or a sacrifice of praise today.

Week 14, Day 4: Special occasions

Sing for joy to God our strength; shout joyfully to the God of Jacob. Raise a song, strike the tambourine, the sweet-sounding lyre with the harp. Blow the trumpet at the new moon, at the full moon, on our feast day. Psalm 81:1-3

The book of Psalms contains music for special occasions such as feast days. For example, Psalm 92 is a prayer for the Sabbath, Psalm 81 is used for the New Moon festival, Psalm 45 was for a wedding (most likely the king's) and Psalms 2 and 110 for a coronation. Psalm 68 was obviously used for a festal celebration (v.24-25). Psalms 120-134, called the Psalms of Ascent, were sung as the people came up to the temple to celebrate the festivals. The Hallel psalms (Ps 113-118) are recited at the end of the Passover Seder meal. Psalm 20 was a liturgy possibly before going to war and Psalms 91 and 121 are both excellent prayers to pray for soldiers and for protection in times of danger.

There are also songs sung on other occasions that are outside of the psalter. Moses and the Israelites sang a song of thanksgiving after the nation was delivered from the Egyptians in Exodus 15:1-18. When the ark was brought up to Jerusalem (1 Chron 16:8-36), there was a great celebration and also at the dedication of the walls in Nehemiah's day (Neh 12:27-43).

The God of the Bible is not one to be relegated to Sunday worship. He wants to be incorporated into every aspect of our lives and included in every occasion we celebrate.

Lord, I choose to make You the centre of every occasion and Lord of every part of my life.

Week 14, Day 5: A psalm for all seasons

The steps of a man are established by the LORD, and He delights in his way. When he falls, he will not be hurled down, because the LORD is the One who holds his hand. Psalm 37:23-24

The whole gamut of human emotion in life in expressed in the book of Psalms, so we can always find something to relate to and use for prayer, or as a model for our own prayers. Some psalms focus on teaching, more like the book of Proverbs, such as Psalms 1, 32, 36, 37 or 119. There is much wisdom to be found in these psalms. David asked for vindication in Psalm 26 and revenge in Psalm 109. However, this side of the cross, we are to forgive our enemies and trust that God will vindicate us (Rom 12:19). David expresses lament and grief at Israel's defeat in war in Psalm 60 and pours out His heart in repentance for his sin in Psalm 51.

Whatever is on our hearts, the lover of our soul rejoices when we share our heart with Him.

One thing I have asked from the LORD, that I shall seek: that I may dwell in the house of the LORD all the days of my life, to behold the beauty of the LORD and to meditate in His temple. For on the day of trouble He will conceal me in His tabernacle; He will hide me in the secret place of His tent; He will lift me up on a rock. Ps 27:4-5

Dear Lord, I come into the secret place today to behold your beauty and meditate on You.

Week 14, Day 6: Prophetic psalms

'But as for Me, I have installed My King upon Zion, My holy mountain.' I will announce the decree of the LORD: *He said to Me, 'You are My Son, today I have fathered You.'* Psalm 2:6-7

One of the responsibilities of the musicians was to prophesy (1 Chron 25:1). The book of Psalms is quoted several times by Jesus and the New Testament writers: Ps 2:2 (Acts 4:25-26), Ps 2:7-8 (Acts 13:33, Heb 5:5), Ps 22:1 (Matt 27:46), Ps 22:18 (Jn 19:24), Ps 31:5 (Lk 23:46), Ps 110:1 (Lk 20:41-44), Ps 110:4 (Heb 5:6), Ps 118:22 (Mk 12:10, Acts 4:11, 1 Pet 2:7). It is clear that the New Testament writers interpreted many of these psalms as prophetic references to the Messiah.

Perhaps surprisingly, Psalm 2 (above) and Psalm 110 (Matt 22:43-45, Acts 2:34-35), 'The LORD said to my Lord, "Sit at my right hand until I put your enemies under your feet"', are the most quoted psalms in the New Testament. Jesus preached the gospel of the Kingdom of God. A kingdom necessitates a king to rule. The Messiah, meaning 'anointed one', originally meant the king, who was anointed at his coronation. The disciples understood that Jesus was the Messiah and that these psalms applied to Him and His Messianic Kingdom. The writer of Hebrews also makes a lengthy explanation of Jesus being the priest 'in the order of Melchizedek' from Psalm 110:4. Jesus' challenge to the Pharisees was to understand that the Messiah was greater than David.

'My God, my God, why have you forsaken me' (Psalm 22:1, Matt 27:46) was originally a liturgy for the dying, but as Jesus quoted from it from the cross, it came to be seen as referring to His death.

Thank You, Jesus, that You are our High Priest without blemish, the fulfilment of the prophetic Scriptures and our coming King who will rule the Messianic Kingdom on earth.

Week 14, Day 7: David's legacy

He [David] left Asaph and his relatives there before the ark of the covenant of the LORD, to minister before the ark continually, as every day's work required. 1 Chron 16:37

God loved the heart of David that wanted to be close to the Lord and for Him to be at the centre of the nation. David could not bear to have the ark of God in Gibeon when he dwelt in Jerusalem, so he built a tent for the ark, before the building of the temple, and appointed musicians to minister before the ark 24/7 (1 Chron 15:16-28, 16:37), reflecting the continuous worship of heaven. Praise and worship were so fundamental to David's life that 288 singers and 4,000 musicians were trained in their skills and taught to prophesy on their instruments (1 Chron 25:1-7). David even made instruments for the musicians to play (1 Chron 23:5)! He organised the Levitical families into 24 divisions that would serve in the temple so the sacrifices and worship would go all year (1 Chron 25:8-31). There was a morning service at dawn and evening sacrifice before dusk, but the incense was to be tended so that it would burn continually, and the fire on the altar was never to go out (1 Chron 23:30-32, Lev 6:12-13). This shows us God's value on worship and prayer. We cannot do this alone, but in groups and communities we can work towards a gathering of people who will keep the fires burning continually.

And the four living creatures, each one of them having six wings, are full of eyes around and within; and day and night they do not cease to say, 'Holy, holy, holy is the LORD God, the Almighty, who was and who is and who is to come.' Rev 4:8

Pray for God to show you others who have a desire and commitment to pray.

Week 15
Praying in tongues

Week 15, Day 1: Promise of the Spirit

These signs will accompany those who have believed: in My name they will cast out demons, they will speak with new tongues; they will pick up serpents, and if they drink any deadly poison, it will not harm them; they will lay hands on the sick, and they will recover. Mark 16:17-18

As part of the great commission given to Jesus' disciples, we are told to go into all the world and preach the gospel to all creation. The signs quoted above would follow the believers, including speaking in new tongues. The following verses note that the disciples went out and preached as they were commissioned to do and the signs followed.

The Greek word *glossolalia* is a name given today for 'speaking in unknown languages'. In 1 Corinthians 13:1 Paul mentions tongues of men and of angels. What is the purpose of this? Paul says:

For the one who speaks in a tongue does not speak to people, but to God; for no one understands, but in his spirit, he speaks mysteries... The one who speaks in a tongue edifies himself; but the one who prophesies edifies the church. 1 Cor 14:2,4

Do you need your spirit to be lifted up today? God is Spirit, and speaking in tongues to God is spirit to Spirit communication. God offers us this gift for our edification.

If you already have this gift, use it today to pray. If not, ask God to grant it to you for your own edification. You may find your prayer life is transformed!

Week 15, Day 2: The day of Pentecost

And they were all filled with the Holy Spirit and began to speak with different tongues, as the Spirit was giving them the ability to speak out. Acts 2:4

When Jesus ascended to heaven, He told the disciples to wait in Jerusalem until the outpouring of the Holy Spirit. This dramatically happened on the Jewish festival of Shavuot (Weeks), fifty days after Passover. The Holy Spirit came as the sound of a rushing, mighty wind, tongues of fire and speaking in new languages which they did not know. Peter most likely preached in Hebrew or Aramaic but it was heard in the many earthly languages that those Jews visiting for the feast recognised and understood.

And how is it that we each hear them in our own language to which we were born?...we hear them speaking in our own tongues of the mighty deeds of God. Acts 2:8, 11

From the 3,000 saved that day, the church of Jesus was born, firstly of Jews in Jerusalem and later also of Gentiles, starting when Peter preached in the house of Cornelius.

While Peter was still speaking these words, the Holy Spirit fell upon all those who were listening to the message. All the Jewish believers who came with Peter were amazed, because the gift of the Holy Spirit had also been poured out on the Gentiles. For they were hearing them speaking with tongues and exalting God. Acts 10:44-46

Thank You, Lord, that You desire both Jews and Gentiles to be filled with your Holy Spirit and speak in tongues. Pour it out on me today, I pray, so that I may exalt You.

Week 15, Day 3: Gifts of the Spirit

But a natural person does not accept the things of the Spirit of God, for they are foolishness to him; and he cannot understand them, because they are spiritually discerned. But the one who is spiritual discerns all things...But we have the mind of Christ. 1 Corinthians 2:14-16

Spiritual gifts are not natural giftings, although they can overlap. There is nothing to say that a trained doctor or surgeon cannot receive a supernatural gift of healing. His job would be made much easier if he did! We can and should use our natural talents and resources for the Kingdom of God. But above and beyond that are the supernatural gifts that bring glory to Jesus because they cannot be explained. A word of knowledge given by a total stranger that pinpoints the cause of a problem, or a word of wisdom that provides an answer, is a gift from heaven. A divine healing of cancer by the laying on of hands, without medical intervention, is a glorious answer to prayer which doctors cannot explain except as a miracle.

Spiritual discernment is something we all need. Jesus accepted that the demonic realm was real, and He cast the demons out. In the power of the Holy Spirit, we can also discern the spiritual powers behind the natural world and overcome them by the blood of the Lamb, the word of our testimony and not loving our lives unto death (Rev 12:11). We are entering very testing days, when Satan is unleashing all his dark forces in the world and evil is rising beyond all we have seen before. We can expect and pray for God to pour out a spiritual revival of prayer and Holy Spirit power to counter this.

Lord, give me the gift of discernment and the mind of Christ to stand in the evil day.

Week 15, Day 4: The gift of tongues

... and to another the effecting of miracles, and to another prophecy, and to another the distinguishing of spirits, to another various kinds of tongues, and to another the interpretation of tongues. 1 Corinthians 12:10

In 1 Corinthians chapter 12, Paul outlines many different spiritual gifts that are given to the body of Christ 'for the common good' (v.7) – wisdom, knowledge, faith, healing, miracles, prophecy, discernment of spirits, tongues and interpretation of tongues. Later in the chapter, he lists again God's appointed leadership areas for the body of Christ as: apostles, prophets, teachers, miracles, healings, helps, administrations and various kinds of tongues (v.27-28). He then goes on to say that they are not all distributed to one person but to different people (v.29-30). He concludes by imploring us to desire and seek the (greater) gifts, especially prophecy.

Paul implies that the church needs all of these gifts of the Holy Spirit to function properly. Unfortunately, some denominations have taught that the gift of tongues was only for the first apostles, as if the church does not need it any more. Surely, we should not refuse a gift God offers us for our edification and that of the church! We know we need wisdom, discernment, healing, faith and miracles, so why not prophecy, tongues and interpretation? In our age of science, repeatable physical evidence is revered above spiritual wisdom. Miracles can't be easily replicated, and tongues is a spiritual gift, not a physical one. God works in a greater realm of reality than human knowledge, so to receive it we must be open to spiritual reality. The evidence will be seen by the results in the lives of individuals and their testimonies.

Father, I am cautious about this because I lack understanding, but I trust that your gifts are always good. Lead and guide me, I pray, into your reality based on your Word.

Week 15, Day 5: Order in the church

I thank God, I speak in tongues more than you all; nevertheless, in church I prefer to speak five words with my mind so that I may instruct others also, rather than ten thousand words in a tongue. 1 Corinthians 14:18-19

1 Corinthians chapter 14 is a key chapter about the right and wrong use of tongues. Paul desires that we all speak in tongues, yet he appears to differentiate between the private and public use of tongues. Privately, it seems that Paul uses tongues frequently to communicate with God in prayer, but in a public meeting or service, he is very clear that interpretation is needed. He states that on such occasions, he would choose to prophesy rather than speak in tongues, for the edification of all present.

It appears that the believers in Corinth were abusing the gifts. Order is needed in the church, so Paul is setting guidelines. A word in tongues should be judged by the prophets. He cautions them to be mindful that all are edified. Instruction through teaching, revelation, word of knowledge or interpreted tongues is more beneficial in a meeting. I am sure we would all agree.

However, one has to speak out a message in tongues before knowing if anyone can interpret, unless there is someone present who has this particular gift. It is therefore preferable for people to learn this gift in small groups before using it in the larger congregation.

Father, please help me to learn to use all your gifts in my own private prayer and in small groups to edify and uplift both myself and other people.

Week 15, Day 6: Paul and tongues

Now I wish that you all spoke in tongues but rather that you would prophesy and greater is the one who prophesies than the one who speaks in tongues, unless he interprets, so that the church may receive edification. 1 Corinthians 14:5

Paul's heart was to see all believers speaking in tongues, interpreting the tongues and prophesying for the good of the church. Have we devalued these gifts? He not only wanted to see people 'receive Jesus into their hearts' but see them baptised and filled with the Holy Spirit.

When Paul came to Ephesus, he found some believers who had been baptised into the baptism of repentance that John had taught but they had not heard of the Holy Spirit. Paul explained that John had foretold of one greater to come, namely Jesus, in whom they should believe.

And when Paul had laid hands upon them, the Holy Spirit came on them and they began speaking with tongues and prophesying. Acts 19:6

We can conclude from this that tongues and prophecy are genuine manifestations of the Holy Spirit. While Jesus said before His ascension that the Holy Spirit would be given in order to be witnesses for Him (Acts 1:8), it is clear from the great commission, that signs, including tongues, were also to accompany that witness (Mk 16:17). Let us not despise any of the gifts of the Spirit but rather pray and ask for, encourage and use the precious spiritual gifts that God promises us so as to be effective witnesses and ministers of the gospel to our brothers and sisters in Christ and in the lost world.

Lord, I am eager to receive all the gifts that You have to offer. Fill me with your Spirit, and let the gifts flow to me and through me to others to your glory. In Jesus' name, I pray.

Week 15, Day 7: The greatest gift is love

If I speak with the tongues of mankind and of angels, but do not have love, I have become a noisy gong or a clanging cymbal. 1 Corinthians 13:1

Right in the middle of Paul's two chapters about spiritual gifts is the beautiful chapter on love. Even more than seeking the spiritual gifts of God, he exhorts us to pursue love. Without this, all the miracles in the world will ring hollow. In heaven, the gifts will not be needed and so will pass away, but love will remain. Tongues will cease, along with prophecy and knowledge (v.8).

If we do not have the character of God, we will not be a useful vessel to demonstrate the gifts, as we are too likely to abuse the gifts through corruption. If our hearts are not pure, we will probably take the glory for ourselves or bring shame to the name of the Lord through our pride. Blasphemy is dishonouring the name of the Lord through our ungodly behaviour. The abuse by some people in the church has turned many off even seeking the supernatural gifts of God. Some denominations have even officially banned the demonstration of such gifts because of failure to discern and address the abuse. This is sad, as it is throwing the baby out with the bathwater. Paul did not ban tongues because the Corinthian services had become unruly. He gave godly wisdom and guidance.

God is supernatural and wants us to be close to Him and work with Him to bring the supernatural realm to earth with love.

Father, fill me with this agape love that can carry your gifts in the right spirit.

Week 16
Little foxes

Week 16, Day 1: Respectable sins

There are six things that the LORD hates, seven that are an abomination to Him: haughty eyes, a lying tongue, and hands that shed innocent blood, a heart that devises wicked plans, feet that run rapidly to evil, a false witness who declares lies, and one who spreads strife among brothers. Proverbs 6:16-19

If God says that something is an abomination to Him or that He hates something, we had better take note. There are big sins like the taking of innocent life, idolatry, child sacrifice (abortion), homosexuality, and giving false witness, but there are also many less obvious ones: selfishness, greed, indulgence, resentment, unbelief, unforgiveness, pride, judgementalism, comparing oneself with others, independence, gossip, putting others down, jealousy, stinginess, lack of compassion, worry, anger, impatience, short-temper, self-pity, self-righteousness, dishonesty, ingratitude – and the list goes on. We may try to justify some of these, but the Bible calls them sin. These are the little foxes that spoil the crops (Song of Sol 2:15).

If we always insist that we are right, then we are not humble. This controlling, demanding attitude destroys relationships. It is rooted in pride and selfishness. We must always be open to correction and accept it with grace without retaliating or getting our heckles up. Manipulation to get our own way is just as destructive.

Prayer is our most powerful weapon, coupled with trusting God to bring the answer. Let us not try to hide from God with 'respectable sins' but be honest before Him. He is for us and wants to take us deeper into the ocean of His love.

Dear Lord, show me any little foxes that need to be removed from my life.

Week 16, Day 2: Worldliness

I find then the principle that evil is present in me, the one who wants to do good. Romans 7:21

We are in a constant war – the war between the flesh and the spirit. Paul cries out in Romans chapter 7 that he finds himself doing the things that he does not want to do. His mind tells him one thing, but his bodily desires want to take over. In many ways, those in the Western churches are indistinguishable from the world. We squabble, we grumble, we love our entertainment and sport, we desire more wealth, we overeat and believe we 'deserve' it because we have worked hard to earn it. There is nothing wrong with wealth and enjoying the blessings of God. However, we need to hold these lightly and be prepared to share them with the needy or forgo them should God ask us to. In the Middle East, hospitality and generosity are highly valued.

No one can serve two masters; for either he will hate the one and love the other, or he will be devoted to one and despise the other. You cannot serve God and wealth. Matt 6:24

It is the fruit of the Spirit that we should be yearning to see maturing in our lives, not the things for which the world craves. We will soon move on to praying for others but before we do, let us go deeper and assess our own lives. Is my life really different from the world? Is there anything that I idolise above my love for God? Am I willing to let go of all to serve Jesus?

Father, show me anywhere where I am still living a worldly life, not a godly one.

Week 16, Day 3: Apathy

I know your deeds, that you are neither cold nor hot; I wish that you were cold or hot. So, because you are lukewarm, and neither hot nor cold, I will vomit you out of My mouth. Because you say, 'I am rich, and have become wealthy, and have no need of anything,' and you do not know that you are wretched, miserable, poor, blind, and naked. Revelation 3:15-17

Alexander Fraser Tyler, Professor of History in Edinburgh in 1770, is attributed with saying that the cycle of democracy lasts about 200 years and goes through the following stages: bondage, spiritual faith, great courage, liberty, abundance, selfishness, complacency, apathy, dependence and back to bondage again.[1]

Let's face it, we live in luxury that a vast majority of the world can only dream about. If we have any money in the bank, we are better off than hundreds of thousands who live in dire poverty. This abundance tends to lead us into independence from God and apathy in our spiritual lives, especially in our prayer lives. We do not see prayer as the vital hub of our life. We can get by without God and often we do. Jesus advised the church in Laodicea, and us, to buy gold refined by fire from Him, white garments to clothe ourselves and eye salve so we can see clearly (Rev 3:18).

Lord, let me not be blind and naked today but clothed in God's righteousness and awake to my need for You.

Week 16, Day 4: Comfort

And others are the ones sown with seed among the thorns; these are the ones who have heard the word, but the worries of the world, and the deceitfulness of wealth, and the desires for other things enter and choke the word, and it becomes unfruitful. Mark 4:18-19

In the parable of the sower, much of the seed did not fall into good soil but was trampled, devoured or choked before it could produce a harvest. Are we producing fruit or just being comfortable? For the sake of the gospel, Paul endured beatings, imprisonment, being stoned, shipwrecked, dangers from both natural and human sources, sleepless nights, hunger, thirst and emotional concern (2 Cor 11:23-28). What am I willing to endure for the sake of the gospel?

Most of us spend many hours per week watching TV, playing games on the internet or chatting on social media. One African pastor commented that everyone in the West has a watch, but no one has the time. In Africa, his people don't have watches, but they do have the time – to pray.

We are very distracted with the busyness of life. There are so many demands on our time, but surely, we have created some of these ourselves, and they could be culled down. Often, if we take those stressful situations to prayer, they will be resolved much faster. God will show us how if we ask.

The saints of old spent many hours in prayer. Rees Howells founded a Bible College in Wales which possibly changed the course of WW1I and saved Britain. They prayed day and night to know the mind of Christ and were given specific arrows of prayer which altered strategic decisions in the war.[2] As I write, the whole Middle East is in turmoil. Perhaps we will be called to intercede like this for nations also. We are living in desperate times. Are we ready?

Abba, make me ready to drop whatever is necessary to answer your call to prayer.

Week 16, Day 5: Pride

Trust in the LORD with all your heart and do not lean on your own understanding. In all your ways acknowledge Him, and He will make your paths straight. Do not be wise in your own eyes; fear the LORD and turn away from evil. Proverbs 3:5-7

It was pride that caused Satan to fall from his position as an archangel around the throne of God (Is 14:11-14, Ezek 28:11-17). David's sin with Bathsheba killed two people, but his sin of pride, against the command of God and advice of Joab, killed 70,000 (2 Sam 24:15). Pride, haughtiness and arrogance are serious sins against God.

The fear of the LORD is to hate evil; pride, arrogance, the evil way, and the perverted mouth, I hate. Prov 8:13

We have the privilege in the West of having years of education, and since the World Wide Web, knowledge has become so readily available that we can find the answer to any question instantly. While the knowledge of the world can be wonderful, if we exalt this over the knowledge of God, and allow human wisdom to override the wisdom of God, we are setting a trap for ourselves. God the Creator is the source of true wisdom and knowledge. We have inherited Greek thinking and from it, humanism, which has always sought to replace God as stated in the humanist manifestos. It is so sad that many go into Bible colleges on fire for God and come out having lost faith, led astray by 'liberal' theologians who analyse and dismember the Word, while exalting human intellect. These are those of whom Paul warned Timothy to avoid: 'holding to a form of godliness although they have denied its power...always learning and never able to come to the knowledge of the truth' (2 Tim 3:5, 7).

Father, forgive me for where I have put human reason above your Word and your truth. Rom 1:18-2:16

Week 16, Day 6: Fear of man

They brought a bad report of the land which they had spied out to the sons of Israel, saying, 'The land through which we have gone to spy out is a land that devours its inhabitants; and all the people whom we saw in it are people of great stature.' Numbers 13:32

The children of Israel stood at the border of the land of their godly inheritance, yet those who were sent ahead to spy out the land returned with a negative report of fearsome giants that inhabited the territory. They saw themselves as grasshoppers in comparison (v.33). Only Joshua and Caleb trusted God and had faith that they would overcome the opposition with God's promise and assistance.

There will always be obstacles in our lives that seems way too big for us to handle. The good news is that we are not meant to tackle them alone. If we call on Him, He will answer and make a way where there seems to be no way, because He is the God of the impossible. No giant is too big for Him (Jer 32:17).

These things I have spoken to you so that in Me you may have peace. In the world you have tribulation, but take courage; I have overcome the world. Jn 16:33

If we are to enter the inheritance that God has for us, we have to see things as Joshua and Caleb did. Not to do so can cause us to wander in the desert for forty years, or worse still, to die there.

Dear Lord, give me courage to trust that You are for me and I can overcome the giants. Ps 60:12, Prov 29:25, Rom 8:31

Week 16, Day 7: Taming the tongue

So also the tongue is a small part of the body, and yet it boasts of great things. See how great a forest is set aflame by such a small fire! James 3:5

James tells us that the tongue is like the rudder of a ship that controls the whole body and a fire that can easily destroy another by nasty words or malicious gossip. There are many sins of the tongue such as boasting, lying, slander, criticism, sarcasm, ridicule, insults, blasphemy or unkind or negative words. When we speak to put another person down, incite someone against another or sow dissention, it is not pleasing to God. Sins of speech can be said directly to a person or behind their back. Our politicians habitually degrade those in another party to bring them down or make them look bad. The expression 'Oh my God' has become so widely used that everyone recognises 'OMG' without a thought that it is taking the name of God in vain.

Let no unwholesome word proceed from your mouth, but only such a word as is good for edification according to the need of the moment, so that it will give grace to those who hear. Eph 4:29 (NASB1995)

As believers, we are to take another course – that of building one another up by our speech and sowing encouragement and unity through our words. If we cannot find something good to say, then it is better to keep our mouth shut. Even amongst friends, it is easy to gossip in the form of passing on information 'for prayer', where it may be better to pray the issue through alone.

Father, teach me to bridle my tongue and only speak positive words that glorify You and build up others.

Week 17

Confession

Week 17, Day 1: Recognising our nature

When I kept silent about my sin, my body wasted away through my groaning all day long…I acknowledged my sin to You, and I did not hide my guilt; I said, 'I will confess my wrongdoings to the LORD'; and You forgave the guilt of my sin. Selah. Psalm 32:3,5

The first meaning of confession is to acknowledge that we are sinners. Our nature is to want to overstep the line and get away with a little bit more than we are allotted or allowed. It does not take long for a baby to push the boundaries when they know the word 'no'. We know the law, but how often do we go a bit over the speed limit? Paul explains this problem well.

For I know that good itself does not dwell in me, that is, in my sinful nature. For I have the desire to do what is good, but I cannot carry it out. For I do not do the good I want to do, but the evil I do not want to do—this I keep on doing. Now if I do what I do not want to do, it is no longer I who do it, but it is sin living in me that does it. Rom 7:18-20 (NIV)

We have to be humble enough to see that we are just the same as Paul. To confess is to verbalise something out loud. If we do not acknowledge this, we will never see our need for a saviour. It is therefore the first step to salvation. But there is far more that is needed for us to be truly converted. We need a complete nature overhaul and a new engine put in!

Father, I do realise that I can't help myself because my nature is sinful, and if I am truly honest, I am utterly selfish, even when I try to do good. I need You to operate on me.

Week 17, Day 2: Acknowledging specific sins

One who conceals his wrongdoings will not prosper, but one who confesses and abandons them will find compassion. Proverbs 28:13

The second stage of salvation is admitting the specific sins of which we are guilty. This causes us to bend lower before the Lord and identify the things that we do that are not according to God's laws. It requires that we admit to specifically violating them and are therefore lawbreakers, guilty of sin and worthy of punishment. That is harder to stomach and puts the spotlight on the dark things that we prefer to keep hidden. We need to see ourselves as we really are and keep short accounts with the Lord. Only then can the Holy Spirit meet us in our weakness and begin to transform us into the image of Christ. The good news is that the veil to the inner court has been torn and we can enter into His presence without fear. It is always safe to come and confess our shortcomings, wrongdoings, doubts and fears to the Lord as He will always forgive us.

If we confess our sins, He is faithful and righteous, so that He will forgive us our sins and cleanse us from all unrighteousness. 1 Jn 1:9

Confession helps us to confront and own our weaknesses. Being forgiven lifts a huge weight off our shoulders. The opening verse, says that it will cause us to prosper and find compassion.

Thank You, Lord, that I can always come before You to confess my sins and find your forgiveness.

Week 17, Day 3: Restitution

Speak to the sons of Israel: 'When a man or woman commits any of the sins of mankind, acting unfaithfully against the LORD, and that person is guilty, then he shall confess his sin which he has committed, and he shall make restitution in full for his wrong and add to it a fifth of it, and give it to him whom he has wronged. But if the person has no redeemer to whom restitution may be made for the wrong, the restitution which is made for the wrong must go to the LORD for the priest, besides the ram of atonement, by which atonement is made for him.' Numbers 5:6-8

Confession of sin required not only an admission of guilt but of actually righting the wrong by restoring what had been lost. If one had stolen something or damaged another's property, then that had to be paid for or restored, plus another 20%. We can't just say we are sorry without bringing restitution for the wrong.

When we have wronged God, we can never repay, and so we need the blood of Jesus to cover us, which it thankfully does. The Father is merciful and the great price that Jesus paid by suffering in our place on the cross has made it possible for us to be pronounced 'not guilty'.

Dear Lord, is there some wrong I have done for which I need to make restitution? Is there someone who needs a debt paid, who I can assist, to show them the love of God, as You have done for me?

Week 17, Day 4: Admitting sin to another

Therefore, confess your sins to one another, and pray for one another so that you may be healed. A prayer of a righteous person, when it is brought about, can accomplish much. James 5:16

There is one thing that the Roman Catholic church has retained that most other denominations have abandoned – the confessional. We do not have to go to a church or a priest to confess our sins, but that would be a good place to start. We can also just confide in a spouse, a friend or a trusted mentor. It is humbling and means we have to stop wearing masks to cover our shame. When we truly repent, we make ourselves vulnerable before the Lord or another person. Our question deep down is always, 'Will they still love me when they know who I really am?' If they are genuine, the answer will be 'yes', and the relationship will probably be stronger. One person's willingness to be open and real generally leads to others feeling safe to do the same in a small group.

The context of today's verse refers to one who is sick and seeking healing from the elders. It implies that at least some illnesses are related to sin. This does not necessarily have to be physical. It can also be an emotional, mental or spiritual malaise. Confessing sin is an excellent way to clear away the cobwebs so we can receive all that God has for us.

Lord Jesus, show me if I am wearing masks that need to be taken off. Is there someone You would have me confess something to?

Week 17, Day 5: Confessing our faith

If you confess with your mouth Jesus as Lord, and believe in your heart that God raised Him from the dead, you will be saved; for with the heart a person believes, resulting in righteousness, and with the mouth he confesses, resulting in salvation. Romans 10:9-10

There is a second meaning to confession used in Scripture. It is also an essential part of the process of salvation. We have to be willing to make public our allegiance to Jesus. Being a secret believer is not an option. That is easily said in the West, but in many countries, it can mean being ostracised from the family or the community, losing one's job, or even death.

The test John gave for discerning between true and false spirits is that they were willing to confess that Jesus has come in the flesh (1 Jn 4:2-3). There are many today who claim that all religions lead to God. The One World religion is a conglomerate of about a dozen. However, the Bible says that only those who will confess that Jesus is the Son of God really belong in His family (1 Jn 2:23, 4:15). This is the decisive point that separates true from false religions. The Arabic writing around the Dome of the Rock on Temple Mount in Jerusalem specifically quotes one verse from the Quran that states that Allah is one and he has no son.

By this you know the Spirit of God: every spirit that confesses that Jesus Christ has come in the flesh is from God; and every spirit that does not confess Jesus is not from God; this is the spirit of the antichrist…and now it is already in the world. 1 Jn 4:2-3

Pray: Let's hold firmly to the confession of our hope without wavering, for He who promised is faithful. Heb 10:23

Week 17, Day 6: Confession in heaven

Now I say to you, everyone who confesses Me before people, the Son of Man will also confess him before the angels of God; but the one who denies Me before people will be denied before the angels of God. Luke 12:8-9

We see from this verse, just how important confessing Jesus before people on earth is. If we are ashamed of our faith and not willing to speak up because others may mock us, think we are crazy or for fear of being rejected, then Jesus will deny us in heaven. This does not mean that we have to make ourselves a pain to be around, but it does mean that we should not allow ourselves to be silenced. If people are doing or saying ungodly things, we need to speak up and make our voice heard in a loving and gentle way. Don't try to shout down the loudmouth but ask a question to make them think. Pray for opportunities to witness and take any that arise. You may well find that your step of courage will embolden others to speak up also. You may also be surprised that when others are in trouble, they will begin to come to you for help.

The one who overcomes will be clothed the same way, in white garments; and I will not erase his name from the book of life, and I will confess his name before My Father and before His angels. Rev 3:5

Thank You, Lord that my good deeds are recorded in your book for eternity.

Week 17, Day 7: Every tongue will confess

For this reason, also, God highly exalted Him, and bestowed on Him the name which is above every name, so that at the name of Jesus every knee will bow, of those who are in heaven and on earth and under the earth, and that every tongue will confess that Jesus Christ is Lord, to the glory of God the Father. Philippians 2:9-11

One day every tongue in heaven and on earth will confess that Jesus is Lord. Is that not encouraging? All the people of the earth will bow before Him and acknowledge His sovereignty. What a glorious day that will be! How the Father will be glorified when heaven and earth join together in praise. I assume this will happen during the thousand-year reign described in Revelation 20:1-6, when Satan is bound.

Blessed and holy is the one who has a part in the first resurrection; over these the second death has no power, but they will be priests of God and of Christ, and will reign with Him for a thousand years. Rev 20:6

Note that those reigning with Him as priests during this period are the martyrs who have given their lives because they belong to Jesus. They are rewarded with this special honour. If I ever have to come to this point, I can only pray God will give me the strength to endure to the end.

And they overcame him because of the blood of the Lamb and because of the word of their testimony, and they did not love their life even when faced with death. Rev 12:11

Dear Lord, I know that I do not have the strength yet to withstand such persecution, but I pray that I will never deny You, and that You will give me the courage when I need it.

Week 18

Perseverance

Week 18, Day 1: The persistent widow

...will God not bring about justice for His elect who cry out to Him day and night, and will He delay long for them? I tell you that He will bring about justice for them quickly. However, when the Son of Man comes, will He find faith on the earth? Luke 18:7-8

Jesus told us the parable of the persistent widow who was pleading for justice and would not give up. Even though the judge was not righteous, he was worn down by her insistence and gave in to her request. Jesus commended her faith and asked rhetorically, 'how much more would our righteous Judge hear our pleas and act on our behalf'? Every parent has probably experienced the same from their children's nagging for things they want. We need to show God that we do seriously want our prayers answered and are prepared to push past the crowds to touch the hem of His garment to encounter His power like the woman healed of the issue of blood (Mk 5:25-34).

In prayer, we need to not give up but Pray Until Something Happens – PUSH for short. This persistence shows our faith and God honours faith. The strongest contractions are the ones immediately before the birth. It can be the same in prayer. God may take us through a process of sifting to change our hearts as we seek His face on important matters. He may even turn us into becoming the answer!

Dear Lord, help me to keep knocking on your door until I see answers coming for my prayers, especially for salvation, justice and healing for my family and friends.

Week 18, Day 2: Running the race

Do you not know that those who run in a race all run, but only one receives the prize? Run in such a way that you may win. Everyone who competes in the games, exercises self-control in all things. So, they do it to obtain a perishable wreath, but we, an imperishable. 1 Corinthians 9:24-25

During his second missionary journey, Paul spent 18 months in Corinth. He became familiar with the culture, which included hosting the biannual Isthmus Games. This drew athletes from many countries and was second only to the Olympic Games. As we know, one does not become a sports star with a casual commitment. Years of training and sacrifice are required to make it to elite standard.

Hebrew culture is not so big on celebrating birthdays and certainly in the Bible, birthdays were not a time of joy for Jews (Gen 40:20-23, Matt 14:6-12). However, the angels were rejoicing when Jesus was born (Lk 2:8-14). It is not how we start that is important, but rather how we run the race of life to we make it successfully to the finish line. This requires not a sprint but a marathon, with many ups and downs. Life is sometimes not even fair and it is easy to want to take off our running shoes and choose the wide path of least resistance. But as we go through hardship, we strengthen our spiritual muscles, just as an athlete strengthens their physical ones and we will see the rewards for our persistence. There is not just a prize awaiting us at the end, but also smaller victory wreaths along the way.

Heavenly Father, help me not to baulk at the hurdles along the path, but to embrace the challenges as training for greater victories.

Week 18, Day 3: The test of endurance

Consider it all joy, my brothers and sisters, when you encounter various trials, knowing that the testing of your faith produces endurance. And let endurance have its perfect result, so that you may be perfect and complete, lacking in nothing. James 1:2-4

I have been told by friends who have run marathons, that there is a point they call 'hitting the wall'. It is the place at which you think you have nothing left and can go no further. At that point, most people give up. However, if you can push through that barrier, you discover that the body can produce more, and the thrill of success is that you actually made it to the end!

The Bible warns us that in the end days, there will be many believers who fall away because of trials and persecution. The early Christians certainly knew about that, and today under many regimes, Christians are persecuted and killed on a daily basis, with Nigeria, North Korea and Myanmar being some of the worst examples. Brother Yun, who spent years in jail in China, tells us to pray that their backs may be strengthened rather than that the persecution be eased, as persecution makes the church stronger.

Gold is refined by fire. The heat gets rid of the dross and the smelting process brings out the pure gold. The goldsmith knows that the process is finished when he can see his reflection in the ingot. Are we reflecting His glory? Can we stand in the day of trial (Mal 3:1-3)?

And some of those who have insight will fall, to refine, purge, and cleanse them until the end time; because it is still to come at the appointed time. Dan 11:35

Dear Lord, keep me strong through the trials and let me not despise the purging process.

Week 18, Day 4: The ANZACs

Suffer hardship with me, as a good soldier of Christ Jesus. No soldier in active service entangles himself in the affairs of everyday life, so that he may please the one who enlists him. 2 Timothy 2:3-4

On April 25, we commemorate ANZAC day, when we remember the soldiers from Australia and New Zealand who fought together in WWI and WWII. They were all volunteers who left homes, families, jobs and loved ones to serve their country on the battlefields, mostly on the other side of the world. Once enlisted, they were expected to stay for the duration of the war and to lay down their lives if need be. It took not months but years, and thousands were scarred for life or never returned. They became renowned for their courage, sacrifice, endurance and mateship, together with their uncanny humour through all the difficulties. These character qualities were forged in battle and helped to form the Australian identity.

We are called to be a spiritual Anzac army with the Lord as our commander-in-chief, leading us into battle and on to victory. Today's youth have fortunately not known war and, as a result, also know little if anything other than gratifying the lusts of the flesh. The Lord needs His warriors to be trained and ready for battle, especially those under forty, who always shoulder the brunt of the workload in times of war.[1]

Abba Father, train me up to be a good soldier for You, equipped and ready to respond to your call.

Week 18, Day 5: Finding joy

Therefore, since we also have such a great cloud of witnesses surrounding us, let's rid ourselves of every obstacle and the sin which so easily entangles us, and let's run with endurance the race that is set before us, looking only at Jesus, the originator and perfecter of the faith, who for the joy set before Him endured the cross, despising the shame, and has sat down at the right hand of the throne of God. Hebrews 12:1-2

The key to endurance is keeping our eyes fixed on the goal ahead. This is how the writer of Hebrews explains that Jesus managed to endure the agony of the cross on our behalf. If we look sideways or behind, we will not make it, but with our eyes on Jesus we can. The Lord will be far more glorified in our trials if we overcome, than in the good times (1 Pet 1:6-7). That is when we learn the peace that passes all understanding and a faith that is not tossed around by the winds of change (Phil 4:7, Jas 1:6).

Jesus is at the right hand of the Father praying for us and there is a cloud of witnesses who are cheering us on in Heaven. If our focus is there, the trials of the world will diminish in their power to overwhelm us. Furthermore, He knows our limitations:

He will not allow you to be tempted beyond what you are able, but with the temptation will provide the way of escape also, so that you will be able to endure it. 1 Cor 10:13

When you pass through the waters, I will be with you; and through the rivers, they will not overflow you. When you walk through the fire, you will not be scorched, nor will the flame burn you. Is 43:2

Thank You, Jesus, for praying me through trial and temptation and helping me to endure.

Week 18, Day 6: Finishing well

I have fought the good fight, I have finished the course, I have kept the faith; in the future there is reserved for me the crown of righteousness, which the Lord, the righteous Judge, will award to me on that day; and not only to me, but also to all who have loved His appearing. 2 Timothy 4:7-8

Paul wrote his own epitaph in his letter to Timothy. What a wonderful way to near the end of his life on earth, being confident that he had completed the work God had for him in this world. Jesus, of course, could also say the same in John chapter 17. What about us?

There is a victory crown that awaits us, as we overcome. To overpower an enemy, we need to engage in battle, not opt out. Our battle is not against flesh and blood but against spiritual powers of darkness (Eph 6:12). As listed in Ephesians 6:13-17, we have been given weapons to fight this battle in the heavenlies. In the days of the anti-Christ:

They overcame him because of the blood of the Lamb and because of the word of their testimony, and they did not love their life even when faced with death. Rev 12:11

Dear Lord, I know that death no longer has any sting, for You have overcome this foe on the cross. Help me not to fear death but to rejoice in the eternal life I have in You.

Week 18, Day 7: Joining the Saints

Do not fear what you are about to suffer. Behold, the devil is about to throw some of you into prison, so that you will be tested, and you will have tribulation for ten days. Be faithful until death, and I will give you the crown of life. Revelation 2:10

Church history tells us that the early Christian community in Smyrna (to whom the above verses were written) did indeed suffer great persecution. Bishop Polycarp was martyred there in 160 CE. Not only in ancient history but also in modern times Christians were hunted down and killed there. In 1922, the Ottoman Turks set fire to the Armenian and Greek quarters of the city which burnt for 10 days (as foretold above). As a result, 100,000 were killed.[2]

The believers in Philadelphia (Rev 3:7-13) were told they would be kept from the hour of testing because they had endured patiently (Rev 3:10-11). However, they still needed to hold fast so as not to lose their crown.

For you have need of endurance, so that when you have done the will of God, you may receive what was promised. For yet in a very little while, He who is coming will come, and will not delay. Heb 10:36-37

Lord Jesus, your coming is getting closer every day. May I hold fast and persevere until your arrival or I am taken to be with You.

The Many Facets of Prayer

Section 2

Praying with and for others

Week 19
Prayer meetings

Week 19, Day 1: Individual and group prayer

They were continually devoting themselves to the apostles' teaching and to fellowship, to the breaking of bread and to prayer. Acts 2:42

We are not only to pray ourselves individually but we are to meet corporately for teaching, fellowship, prayer and communion as in Acts 2:42. As individuals, we are free to begin and end as we are led and just follow the Holy Spirit's promptings. When we are in a group situation, we need to be aware of what the flow of the Spirit is for the group and not just butt in with what is on our heart at the time. We need to seek agreement with others in the group, as it is in unity that the Spirit of God gives His blessing.

Behold, how good and how pleasant it is for brothers to live together in unity!...For the LORD commanded the blessing there – life forever. Ps 133:1, 3c

It is encouraging in a group to have people respond with a prayer along similar lines or an 'Amen' of agreement at the end. While times of quiet are appropriate on some occasions, it is not much point coming together to sit in silence and pray alone. Corporate prayer should be interactive, so ask the Lord before the meeting, as well as during, what He would have you contribute. We are to be a body, not just a lot of followers, relying on the leader to hear from God.

Prepare yourself before you attend the next prayer meeting and see what God will give you to contribute to the meeting.

Week 19, Day 2: The flow of the Holy Spirit

When you assemble, each one has a psalm, has a teaching, has a revelation, has a tounge, has an interpretation. All things are to be done for edification. 1 Corinthians 14:26

A prayer gathering is to be a time of edification, of building up the body. If members are trained to come with a word or a song or a revelation to share, then this is a launching pad for the meeting. When each has had a chance to share briefly (not preach a sermon!), then we will all get a sense of where the Spirit is taking us for the meeting. Unfortunately, most often the sheep simply rely on the shepherd or prayer leader to do the listening for them. Prayer meetings should not replace our own private times of prayer but should supplement them. It can be helpful to have a short teaching, but often these become a lecture with little practical prayer participation. We all learn best by guided, hands-on practice rather than text-book instruction.

As we share our hearts before one another and God, we are brought into unity and the Holy Spirit can flow amongst us as a river of life. It is important that we learn to listen to the whispers of God and be sensitive to the Holy Spirit. Sometimes the quietest people have the deepest revelations that we all need to hear.

A plan in the heart of a person is like deep water, but a person of understanding draws it out. Prov 20:5

At your next prayer meeting, encourage the quiet ones to share their thoughts and revelations.

Week 19, Day 3: Prayer partners and mentors

Again I say to you, that if two of you agree on earth about anything that they may ask, it shall be done for them by My Father who is in heaven. Matthew 18:19

Prayer partners are a wonderful gift. When two or three people come together in agreement, God promises to grant their wishes. By adding one or two people, we actually multiply our effectiveness. A prayer partner is someone who is of one heart with us in seeking to do the Father's will and with whom we can share our heart's desires in the spiritual realm. Your prayer partner may be your husband or wife or a trusted friend or two. It is also good to bounce off one another to check things out, especially when it comes to interpreting words, visions or dreams. It also allows us to complement one another with our different gifts, encouraging and strengthening one another. Another benefit is accountability so that we do not veer off track.

If you are seeking to grow in prayer or any aspect of ministry, it is also helpful to ask a person more experienced and gifted in that area to mentor and pray for you and with you as you grow. Practical experience and observance as you follow the teacher is the way Jesus' disciples learnt.

Dear Lord, do You have someone with whom I could pray as a prayer partner or mentor?

Week 19, Day 4: Small groups

With every prayer and request, pray at all times in the Spirit, and with this in view, be alert with all perseverance and every request for all the saints, and pray in my behalf, that speech may be given to me in the opening of my mouth, to make known with boldness the mystery of the gospel, for which I am an ambassador in chains; that in proclaiming it I may speak boldly, as I ought to speak. Ephesians 6:18-20

Most churches have one prayer meeting per week, perhaps supplemented with a shorter time to pray before the service on Sundays. Typically, this is attended by a handful of people, mostly elderly women. Sadly, in the West, the prayer meeting is often the least attended church meeting for the week. In Africa and South Korea, things are vastly different.

Prayer was the key to Jesus' life and ministry, and until we see this as the hub of the church's ministry, we will not see breakthrough. Paul calls us to pray at all times. If our works are not seeded from heaven, they will not accomplish anything for the Kingdom of God.

It is good and necessary to pray for the services and ministries of the congregation, but our focus is not to be on ourselves. Every ministry of the church should have its own prayer support and be couched in prayer. As well as that, we need prayer meetings for specific purposes such as outreach, families, missions, the persecuted church, the government and Israel. If God lays one of these on your heart, then seek to find at least one other who will join you. There are such groups that pray online regularly for these things. What Satan meant for bad with Covid lockdowns has led to an explosion in online national and global prayer!

Seek to find others who will join you in praying for these wider issues of concern.

Week 19, Day 5: Public prayer

For you can all prophesy one by one, so that all may learn and all may be exhorted; and the spirits of prophets are subject to prophets; for God is not a God of confusion, but of peace. 1 Corinthians 14:31-33

Paul's idea of a congregational meeting was not that one person dominates the time but rather that a number of people share their gifts to edify, exhort or console each other (1 Cor 14:3, 26). He is concerned that there be order (1 Cor 14:40) but also that the gifts are not quenched (1 Thess 5:19-21).

These principles also apply to public prayer. Leaders need to guard the space but also allow the Spirit to flow. They should seek to foster unity and a welcoming, loving spirit within the congregation. The gifts of tongues must be interpreted in public meetings (1 Cor 14:5, 13). Manipulation or domination should not be tolerated in the public place as this can lead the young believers or unbelievers astray. Gentle but firm correction is needed.

We see quite a few political rallies against ungodly laws that are being passed in our parliaments. While it is good to make a public stance, it would be even more beneficial to see more prayer rather than just a parade of speakers at these gatherings. Prayer changes the atmosphere in the heavenly realm, and when we declare His Word over our cities and parliaments, it can be a powerful tool for change.

If you are an introverted person, pray that God will give you the courage to pray aloud in public. If you are an extrovert and like to lead, pray to develop the gift of listening.

Week 19, Day 6: The abuse of prayer

For lack of wood the fire goes out, and where there is no gossiper, quarrelling quiets down. Like charcoal to hot embers and wood to fire, so is a contentious person to kindle strife. Proverbs 26:20-21

A prayer meeting is meant to be a time of meeting with God to listen to Him together. This is not the time for people to chatter with private conversations. We need to be disciplined when we come together, listening to what others and the Holy Spirit are saying. If we are not the leader, it is not our job to direct the meeting or to use the platform to preach or teach. Unfortunately, Satan sometimes plants people in our congregations who refuse to die to self and wish to dominate and control wherever they are, including in prayer meetings. They are prone to long prayers that go from one topic to the next without stopping for breath and refuse to stick to the topic that may be the focus of the prayer time.

Another abuse of the prayer time is to use prayer to pass on information that is not known publicly regarding situations that may be private, especially without the relevant person's consent. This can amount to gossiping. Another danger is using prayer to manipulate the behaviour or will of others. God gives us free will. He will not take that away from us, nor should we demand of Him to do that to others. It is better to pray that He would draw them to Himself, soften their hearts and that they would be open to hear and obey God's voice.

Lord, show me if I have prayed controlling prayers or tried to manipulate others or spoken words that are out of order. I repent for not following your Holy Spirit or grieving You with such words or actions.

Week 19, Day 7: Leading prayer meetings

Now give me wisdom and knowledge, so that I may go out and come in before this people, for who can rule this great people of Yours? 2 Chronicles 1:10

Solomon prayed that he might have wisdom to lead the people. This should be the prayer for every leader in the church. In God's Kingdom, leadership is about serving and equipping the people, not lording it over them (Lk 22:25-26).

In prayer meetings, people need to be taught to pray short prayers, to the point and stay on one topic. Encourage others who have the same topic on their heart to also express their prayer. Keep on track and finish one topic before moving on to another. Ask the quiet ones if they have something to share. Don't allow one person to dominate or manipulate the meeting and don't do so yourself as leader.

As leader, it is vital that you prepare before the meeting by spending time with the Lord and asking His direction for the meeting. Be prepared to lead but also to change direction if the Holy Spirit goes elsewhere. Listen to what He is saying through others in the meeting and encourage the full participation of the Body of Christ. It is also helpful to draw the threads together and summarise what the Spirit is saying.

Teach me, Lord to be able to sensitively lead others as we pray together, to hear what You are saying and to give You all the thanks and glory.

The Many Facets of Prayer

Week 20
Pastoral prayer

Week 20, Day 1: More, Lord

For from days of old they have not heard or perceived by ear, nor has the eye seen a God besides You, who acts in behalf of one who waits for Him.
Isaiah 64:4

The most exciting prayer meetings I have ever attended have been where there was a good half hour of praise and worship at the start and the Lord was invited to share His heart with us. People were taught to listen to the Holy Spirit and share what they were seeing and hearing. As participants shared, often a theme emerged, and the group was then invited to pray into what God was saying through the Scriptures, visions, words, testimonies or songs. This is not your normal boring prayer list where people rarely see many answers, but a sacred place where heaven and earth meet in one accord.

Typically, in our church prayer meetings, the sick ones in the church are prayed for, the various ministries are brought before the Lord, and the Lord's blessings are sought for the services and any upcoming events of the church. It is rarely the hub around which everything else revolves. This is usually the extent of knowledge most people ever learn about prayer and is one main reason for writing this devotional. There is nothing wrong with this type of pastoral prayer. It is needed, but there is so much more to prayer that is rarely explored.

With modern technology, many churches now use social media apps (WhatsApp, Signal, Telegram or similar) to inform intercessors of needs for which they pray from home or wherever they are. It is quick, easy to access and can immediately raise up effective prayer for urgent needs. However, we must not neglect meeting together, as it has a multiplying effect.

Lord, show us the most effective ways to pray and help us use all resources to maximum benefit for your Kingdom.

Week 20, Day 2: Love one another

I am giving you a new commandment, that you love one another; just as I have loved you, that you also love one another. By this all people will know that you are My disciples: if you have love for one another. John 13:34-35

The church is meant to be a family where everyone is welcome and accepted. Jesus said the world will know Him as we love one another. Many church buildings are unfortunately set up more like theatres with the performers at the front and the audience at the back. The formality of many services is also not conducive to participation. The early church met in homes around a dinner table and shared fellowship, prayer, communion (the meal - including bread and wine) and teaching. These smaller settings are where people begin to know one another and relate in real life. When outsiders see others truly caring for one another in action, they will be drawn to know more of this love.

Jesus' prayer in John 17 was mostly about unity of the brethren. Division in a church will drive the unsaved away. Newcomers desire a warm, hospitable atmosphere where they feel welcome and see the love of the congregants for one another. At the same time, we are not to tolerate what the Lord calls evil. God loves sinners but not their sin. So must we.

Father, bring to my mind anyone You want me to show your love to today. How should I do that? Please make my church a loving and welcoming place for visitors.

Week 20, Day 3: Prayer for the sick

Is anyone among you sick? Then he must call for the elders of the church and they are to pray over him, anointing him with oil in the name of the Lord; and the prayer of faith will restore the one who is sick, and the Lord will raise him up, and if he has committed sins, they will be forgiven him. James 5:14-15

The first place we should run to when sick is Dr Jesus, the Lord our Healer (Ex 15:26). Much of Jesus' ministry involved praying for the sick. His answer to sickness was to pray and command the evil spirits to leave. He attributed illness in some cases to demons (Matt 17:18), sin (Jn 5:14), natural causes (Is 38:1-3) and so that God would be glorified (Jn 9:3). He acted out of compassion, healing all who came to Him (Matt 4:23, 8:16). His authority over disease was a sign of God's anointing (Lk 7:18-23). Illness can be a punishment (1 Sam 5:6), a consequence (Dt 28:21-22), a trial (2 Cor 12:7) or perhaps the result of an accident (Lk 13:4), wear and tear or something in the air. The good news is that Jesus has borne our sicknesses and carried our sorrows and pains and by His wounds we are healed (Is 53:4-5).

He authorised His disciples to continue this ministry and they came back rejoicing (Lk 10:8-9, 17-20). Laying hands on the sick is part of the great commission (Mk 16:17-18) with restoration being a sign of God's Kingdom presence. We can thank God for today's medical advances and not despise those who can help us by human means, but in praying for the sick, we need to discern the root cause, then take the axe to the root. We are assured that if we follow the instructions in James above, that the Lord will hear the prayer of faith and act on our behalf.

Study how Jesus responded to the sick who came to Him. Let this insight direct your payers.

Week 20, Day 4: Male and female

God created man in His own image...male and female He created them. God blessed them; and God said to them, 'Be fruitful and multiply, and fill the earth'... Genesis 1:27-28

The nuclear family of mother, father and children is under threat in the West. The Australian Bureau of Statistics in 2021 reported that nearly 16% of families are lone-parent and nearly 39% have no children. There were just under 24,000 same-sex marriages, 8,747,135 heterosexual marriages, 2,168,351 de facto relationships and 7,863,327 unmarried or single.[1] In addition, an estimated 21% of adults have experienced partner violence or partner emotional or economic abuse since the age of 15.[2]

Many homes are no longer safe places for children. With no mum or no dad or living in a violent household, children have no model of love or natural, loving relationships. This breeds generational brokenness. We need to be praying for the families in our churches to be strong and blessed. We also need to be aware of those inside and outside the church who are struggling with family issues or who have no family support – the elderly, the single parents and the unmarried, who need enfolding into the Father's arms and into the church family.

Fatherlessness is also a huge problem in society. We all need to know the Father's love. Praying together is a fantastic way to bond the family. Those that pray together, stay together.

Lord, bless the families in my church today. Make them strong and loving places where each member is encouraged, built up and supported and comes into a deep relationship with You.

Week 20, Day 5: Lure of the world

For this reason, God will send upon them a deluding influence so that they will believe what is false in order that they all may be judged who did not believe the truth, but took pleasure in wickedness. But we should always give thanks to God for you, brothers and sisters beloved by the Lord, because God has chosen you from the beginning for salvation through sanctification by the Spirit and faith in the truth. 2 Thessalonians 2:11-12

Our youth are under siege from secular and demonic ideologies that lure them away from God and into the lusts of the flesh and self-indulgence. It is a time to be really praying for them for good peer group friends who are morally sound and leaders with strong character who will lead them in the righteous ways of God. Youth groups are so vital in our churches. If these are not well-organised and with sound teaching, the young ones will seek other groups with other values. The university years, and the time for seeking a life partner, are also periods of vulnerability. As young adults, they need to find their own identity and moral compass. The raging hormones want gratification and the world screams at them to be like everyone else. Oh, how they need the wisdom of the book of Proverbs to stay on track! It is the daily prayers of their faithful and caring parents that will undergird them to cross this bridge of life intact and trusting God. Do not underestimate the power of prayer and the necessity of the intercession of the church body for these young people. It can be a tough time of rebellion and rejection of the parental values and even turning away from God but if you train your children in the ways of God and continue to pray, God promises they will not depart from them (Prov 22:6).

Pray for the youth to come to know God and hold fast to their faith when pressured by the world. Pray also for the prodigals to come home. Lk 15:11-32

Week 20, Day 6: Bring in the harvest

Preach the word; be ready in season and out of season; correct, rebuke, and exhort, with great patience and instruction. For the time will come when they will not tolerate sound doctrine; but wanting to have their ears tickled, they will accumulate for themselves teachers in accordance with their own desires, and they will turn their ears away from the truth and will turn aside to myths. 2 Timothy 4:2-4

If you are in a healthy church, it will be reaching out to the lost and disadvantaged in your vicinity in some way. We are not just meant to be a club or humanitarian aid organisation, but to take the message of the gospel of salvation and the Kingdom of God to the world, displaying the manifest love and power of God in word and action. Paul exhorted Timothy to always be ready to preach the Word, and we must be available and praying for opportunities to share His love, pray for those we meet and be ready to explain to them the way of salvation. As the world gets darker, our light must shine brighter. Jesus is the answer, and we must show them this. Be prepared. Get some evangelistic tracts, or write your own and keep them handy.

Pray for the outreach ministry of your church and if there isn't one, consider starting one! Pray for God to raise up and equip those who are gifted in evangelism and uplift them in prayer. Time is short. We urgently need to wake people up that they will be accountable to God for how they live their lives here. Heaven or hell await us and we have one lifetime to decide (Heb 9:27). Jesus wants a full house for the marriage supper of the Lamb (Rev 19:7-9)!

Pray for the harvest of souls to come in.

Week 20, Day 7: The persecuted church

Blessed is a man who perseveres under trial; for once he has been approved, he will receive the crown of life which the Lord has promised to those who love Him. James 1:12

Unfortunately, Greek individualism has pervaded the church and we Christians rarely see ourselves as a global tribe. Amongst Muslims, when the name of Allah is 'defamed' (often by a false allegation) the whole Islamic world reacts and causes a global uproar. Christians are probably the most persecuted ethnic group on the planet – 1 in 7 globally, 1 in 5 in Africa and 2 in 5 in Asia[3], but because the church does not make a noise about it, the media do not bother to report it. Tens of thousands of Christians have been and still are being murdered, imprisoned or displaced because of their faith in Africa, the Middle East and in China.

We need to be praying regularly for our brothers and sisters who are suffering, simply because they hold to Jesus. The Barnabus Fund[4] and Open Doors[5] are two organisations that assist the persecuted church and provide prayer points. The way the world is headed, we in the West may soon be in the same situation. The words of Lutheran pastor Martin Niemöller in the 1930s are so true: "First they came for the socialists, and I did not speak out – because I was not a socialist. Then they came for the trade unionists, and I did not speak out – because I was not a trade unionist. Then they came for the Jews, and I did not speak out – because I was not a Jew. Then they came for me – and there was no one left to speak for me."[6]

Take time today to pray for the Christians around the world who are suffering for their faith. Find an organisation that will keep you in touch with those who need prayer.

The Many Facets of Prayer

Week 21
Prayer shield

Week 21, Day 1: Prayer cover

The LORD is your protector; The LORD is your shade on your right hand. The sun will not beat down on you by day, nor the moon by night. The LORD will protect you from all evil; He will keep your soul. The LORD will guard your going out and your coming in from this time and forever. Psalm 121:5-8

Interceding for others as a prayer shield can be very rewarding, as can allowing others to cover you. It builds relationship and friendship and brings accountability. The Lord Himself is our shield, but we can also be a shield for one another and most certainly should be for our family. It is simply a matter of spending time waiting on the Lord and dedicating some time to pray for others. This is more ongoing than just praying for someone who has a particular need at the time. In most cases, it will result in a word of encouragement to share with the person or a scripture or song. It should not be used to tell the other what to do – that is the Holy Spirit's job – but there is nothing wrong with sharing some wisdom. Just be aware not to coerce or judge the other. Our duty as intercessors is to uplift, not condemn. If the person is in a difficult situation, such prayer cover can be vital. It is good to ask the Lord for a scripture to declare.

We live in times of great deception. Artificial intelligence is mimicking faces and voices and can replicate almost anything to appear real. We can't trust what is said on the news as it is so biased, and there are constantly people trying to trick us into giving them access to our personal information – or stealing it. We all need prayer cover to keep us on track.

Keep watching and praying, so that you will not come into temptation; the spirit is willing, but the flesh is weak. Mk 14:38

Lord, show me who You would have me cover in prayer today.

Week 21, Day 2: Praying for pastors

Be diligent to present yourself approved to God as a worker who does not need to be ashamed, accurately handling the word of truth. 2 Timothy 2:15

Believe it or not, pastors are often very lonely. They spend their time caring for others but often do not receive much care themselves. Many suffer burnout from overwork, trying to look after a congregation and their own family with little time for themselves. They have few, if anybody, to turn to if they have needs and must keep strong for the sake of others who rely on them.

Let no one look down on your youthfulness, but rather in speech, conduct, love, faith, and purity, show yourself an example of those who believe. 1 Tim 4:12

Your pastor may not be young, but the qualities above are good for all of us to practise. Encourage your pastor, and keep praying that he or she will guard their time with the Lord, keep their relationship with Him as their first priority, be anointed and filled with the Spirit of God, overflowing with His love and power to fulfil their calling and bring glory to God. Pray for a team around them which can minister in giftings that are complementary to his or hers and for the true gospel to be preached without compromise.

Thank God for your pastor and pray for him or her today.

Week 21, Day 3: Praying for leaders

Now we ask you, brothers and sisters, to acknowledge those who work hard among you, who care for you in the Lord and who admonish you. Hold them in the highest regard in love because of their work. Live in peace with each other. 1 Thessalonians 5:12-13 (NIV)

Those in leadership positions whether in the church, business or government, are often subject to much more temptation than most of us. Where money, position or power are involved, those who want to profit for their own ends will try to manipulate, threaten or bribe. It takes strong character to stand against these forces, and it can make all the difference if the intercessors are shielding the leaders in prayer.

But those who want to get rich fall into temptation and a trap, and many foolish and harmful desires which plunge people into ruin and destruction. 1 Tim 6:9

We often tend to criticise our leaders and complain about them but we would be far better to spend our breath in turning that into a prayer and upholding them before the Lord.

Lord, I pray for the leaders in my church, workplace, community and government as You bring them to mind. May they come to know You (if they don't already) and to align with your Word and your ways. I pray that You shield them from manipulation and abusing their position and power for selfish ends, and help them always do what is best for the people they are serving.

Week 21, Day 4: Intercessors and pastors

You younger men, likewise, be subject to your elders; and all of you, clothe yourselves with humility towards one another, because God is opposed to the proud, but He gives grace to the humble. Therefore, humble yourselves under the mighty hand of God, so that He may exalt you at the proper time. 1 Peter 5:5-6

Unfortunately, pastors and intercessors do not always get on well together. Intercessors hear from God and can't understand why the pastor does not see what they are seeing and may disregard what they share. It is your job initially to pray about what God has shown you and only to share what and when He directs. We need to beware of pride that can creep in or an attitude that can come across as controlling or manipulating. When we share a word, we are not responsible for how the other person responds to it. It is wise to ask if that gels with the recipient or confirms what they are hearing. It is always possible we may be wrong, or it may be for a future time. If they receive it, great. If not, then we continue to pray and leave it in the Lord's hands. It is more important to keep the relationship with one another than to demand that we are right. Keep humble, and God will exalt you in due time.

Pastors also need to value their intercessors, who pray for them and shield them from attack. God only knows how often danger or deception has been averted due to the faithful prayers of intercessors. Seek to raise up a team who will support you in prayer, and make sure you take the time to thank them and show your appreciation for what they do.

Therefore, encourage one another and build one another up, just as you also are doing. 1 Thess 5:11

Dear Jesus, I ask You for a word of encouragement for my pastor today.

Week 21, Day 5: Those in dangerous jobs

He will cover you with His pinions, and under His wings you may take refuge; His faithfulness is a shield and wall. Psalm 91:4

There are certain vocations that are of necessity more dangerous than others. Our security forces – army, navy, air force and border forces – are at the frontline of our protection from potential invaders. In addition, the police and emergency services are the ones called to deal with natural or man-made incidents. They risk their lives for our safety. They often see death and terrible destruction and that is emotionally upsetting and hard to leave at the office at the end of the day. It is rewarding to see lives saved and people helped out in an emergency, but it can also be confronting when all their best efforts fail.

If you know people serving in these capacities, make it your duty to pray for them daily or at least ask the Lord to alert you for times of specific danger when they need special covering. It may one day be us in the emergency that need their help. If you have been assisted by them, be sure to go back and say thank you. This little gesture keeps them afloat when they are tired and stressed to the limit. Also remember their families who live in constant concern for their safety and often have to endure long periods of separation when they are on duty away from home. We are seeing dramatic increases in the number of cases of Post Traumatic Stress Disorder (PTSD) from former soldiers who have seen active service overseas and returned traumatised.

Father, I lift up our security and emergency services before You today. Consider writing a note of thanks or taking some flowers to your local police, fire or SES station.

Week 21, Day 6: Special assignments

This is what the LORD says: 'Go and buy a potter's earthenware jar, and take some of the elders of the people and some of the senior priests. Then go out to the Valley of Ben-hinnom, which is by the entrance of the Potsherd Gate, and proclaim there the words that I tell you.' Jeremiah 19:1-2

The Lord often calls intercessors to specific assignments. For most of us, they will be prayer assignments, though some may involve going to a specific place to pray, often accompanied by prophetic acts. Very few of us will have to deliver a message as heavy as what Jeremiah had to say. I have led several prayer tours with specific places to visit and assignments to do. These confronted strongholds and also involved praying for the redemptive purposes God had to replace the evil. Where possible, we involved local believers or worked with local intercessors. These required quite a bit of research as well as prayer leading up to them and in training the team that was going, as well as following up afterwards. Such assignments need to be covered by a team back home who will faithfully pray each day for those on the assignment. This is vastly different to a tourist tour and all participants need to understand that and be prepared.

On one recent assignment, we had 25 people on the ground and another 25 on a zoom call around the nation who were praying and worshipping for the four-hour period needed to complete the assignment. This is essential to keep the team on the ground protected spiritually.

Father, please show me how to pray if You call me to participate in such an assignment or to cover someone involved.

Week 21, Day 7: Missionaries

With every prayer and request, pray at all times in the Spirit, and with this in view, be alert with all perseverance and every request for all the saints, and pray in my behalf, that speech may be given to me in the opening of my mouth, to make known with boldness the mystery of the gospel, for which I am an ambassador in chains; that in proclaiming it I may speak boldly, as I ought to speak. Ephesians 6:18-20

Those serving the Lord on the mission field are especially worthy of our prayers. This is frontline pioneering work and Satan will try to hinder any advancement of the gospel. The prayer requested by Paul in the text above, and also by Peter and John, was for boldness in the face of opposition, arrest and imprisonment. Those on the mission field need courage and strength and good health also, especially as they are serving in an unfamiliar environment, often involving a different language and customs. Pray they can find relevant ways to present the gospel that the people can relate to and accept, and for soft hearts to receive the message. This is particularly necessary today, as there is a trend towards the Christian message to indigenous people groups being seen as 'Western' or 'stealing their identity'.

Some on the mission field are also single, which can lead to loneliness, especially when living away from home, friends and support. Pray for God to wrap His arms around them in a special way and be the lover of their souls.

Don't forget those who are serving God in a missionary capacity in their own land, planting churches, raising up new ministries or taking the gospel to unreached or disadvantaged groups within the society.

Lord, I pray for those serving You on mission fields here and in other countries and cultures. Meet their every need and show me how I can support those You bring to my mind.

Week 22
Intercession

Week 22, Day 1: What is intercession?

I searched for a man among them who would build up a wall and stand in the gap before Me for the land, so that I would not destroy it; but I found no one. Ezekiel 22:30

Many people think of intercession as a more intense type of prayer, but it is more. To intercede is to intervene on behalf of another or stand in the gap between two parties. We intercede between God and humans by lifting others up before the throne of God, especially when they are unable to do so themselves because they do not yet know God or they are weak at the time, like the paralysed man in Luke 5:18-25.

In Ezekiel chapter 22, the prophet speaks of the contention that God has with the nation of Israel and warns that He is about to judge them. The false prophets placated the people, the priests no longer distinguished between the holy and the profane, the leaders made dishonest gain and the people robbed from the poor and the stranger. When a nation is in trouble due to such sin, God looks for intercessors to stand in the gap.

Rees Howells noted three characteristics of intercessors that set them apart: identification, agony and authority.[1] The intercessors do not just pray for someone; they go deeper to identify and feel the pain of the one suffering. In praying for a nation, they are repenting for *our* sin not their sin. They share in the agony of bearing the sin or pain on behalf of another to pay for the debt or consequences. In doing so, they gain authority not only for one occasion but for all such situations in that category. God often gives intercessors spiritual assignments or a particular person to pray for, and they then have the responsibility to carry through until that assignment is completed, which could take years. This prayer devotional is such an assignment for me.

Father, help me to be willing to stand in the gap for others or my nation.

Week 22, Day 2: Jesus our intercessor

Jesus, on the other hand, because He continues forever, holds His priesthood permanently. Therefore, He is also able to save forever those who come to God through Him, since He always lives to make intercession for them. Hebrews 7:24-25

Jesus is our perfect example of an intercessor. He was tempted as we are (Heb 2:18), and in His humanity, He suffered all the things we do and learnt obedience through that suffering, but overcame for us (Heb 5:7-10). Through His perfection, He won our eternal salvation. He suffered the agony of the cross, laid down His life for our sin and died our death, paying the price for our freedom (Gal 3:13). He overcame death and now holds the keys to death and Hades (Rev 1:18). He has therefore been given all authority in heaven and earth (Matt 28:18) and is now seated at the right hand of God in the place of perfect intercession for us.

...He raised Him from the dead and seated Him at His right hand in the heavenly places, far above all rule and authority and power and dominion, and every name that is named, not only in this age but also in the one to come. And He put all things in subjection under His feet, and made Him head over all things to the church, which is His body, the fullness of Him who fills all in all. Eph 1:20-23

Heavenly Father, give me a revelation of what You did for me and the authority You gained.

Week 22, Day 3: Abraham

And the Lord said, 'The outcry of Sodom and Gomorrah is indeed great, and their sin is exceedingly grave'…Abraham came near and said, "Will you indeed sweep away the righteous with the wicked? Suppose there are fifty righteous within the city; will You indeed sweep it away and not spare the place for the sake of the fifty righteous who are in it?" Genesis 18:20, 23-24

God was about to judge Sodom and Gomorrah for their grave sin of self-indulgence which was manifest in widespread homosexuality. Abraham was disturbed for this impending doom, especially since his nephew Lot and family lived there. He stood in the gap for the unrighteous, wicked cities and pleaded with God on their behalf. Despite his acknowledgment of his own unworthiness to question God, he argued for the cities to be spared on the grounds of God's merciful nature and just character. In his bargaining with God, he reduced the number to ten, but the Lord could not even find that many. However, He did spare Lot's family.

God was not angry with Abraham for his pleas. We can actually avert adversity through our intercession if we have the heart of God. History is indeed in the hands of the intercessors. He does not want to bring judgement and is slow to anger. Scripture tells us that mercy triumphs over judgement (Jas 2:13b). After all, God sent Jesus so we have a way of escape from the punishment due to us because of our sins. We are called to walk in the same attitude of mercy towards lost sinners.

Father, give me this gift of mercy that sees lost sinners with such compassion. It is your goodness that draws us to repentance. Rom 2:4

Week 22, Day 4: Moses

And on the next day Moses sasid to the people, 'You yourselves have committed a great sin; and now I am going up to the LORD; perhaps I can make attonement for your sin...' 'But now, if You will forgive their sin, very well; but if not, please wipe me out from your book which You have written!' Exodus 32:30, 32

Moses was so heartbroken when he saw the people whom he had led out of slavery so quickly reverting to idol worship that he was willing for God to wipe him out for the sake of his people. He stood in the gap for the people's sin and presented himself before God to seek atonement. God promised to lead the people on but none of that generation would enter the land of their inheritance. They forfeited that blessing to the next generation. The consequence of rejecting God is very high. We need to be interceding passionately for the lost.

This type of prayer needs commitment, as the true intercessor has to be willing to lay down their life for the one for whom he or she is interceding, as Moses offered. We need to love the disobedient and rebellious people, as he did and as Jesus does. It also requires a high level of obedience from leaders. Moses' presumption and lack of trust to strike the rock instead of speaking to it meant he could not enter the land either (Num 20:8-13, 27:14, Dt 32:51-52). The good news is that Jesus' blood is now shed for us and our salvation is assured, but sin still has consequences that may have to be worked through.

Dear Lord, help me to understand the severity of sin and how it hurts You. You did such a deep work on the cross and I need to understand this more to intercede as You did for the lost world.

Week 22, Day 5: David

So Gad came to David that day and said to him, 'Go up, erect an altar to the LORD on the threshing floor of Araunah the Jebusite'...the king said to Araunah, "No, but I will certainly buy it from you for a price; for I will not offer burnt offerings to the LORD my God that cost me nothing." 2 Samuel 24:18,24

David had committed a great sin. His adultery with Bathsheba and murder of her husband affected one family. But David took an unauthorised census (Ex 30:11-16) against the Word of God and his army chief's advice that cost the lives of 70,000 men (2 Sam 24:15). He regretted his foolish arrogance (v.10) and God sent the prophet Gad with His redemption plan.

He had to erect an altar on the land that became the site of the two temples, considered to be the same site where Abraham built the altar to sacrifice Isaac. This meant that David had to purchase the threshing floor from Araunah (i.e. buy his business) and the land it was on. The purpose of an altar is a place to sacrifice. The temple became the central place of sacrifice to intervene between heaven and earth. More importantly, the temple was to be the house of God, His dwelling place on earth and in the holy of holies was the throne of God, His judgement seat. Hence, it will become the throne of Jesus at His return, which is why Satan is desperate to gain Temple Mount as his throne.

David's disobedience had a high cost. He paid the price to stop the plague, bought the land and prepared everything for his son Solomon to build the house of God. In intercession, we are also paying the price to see the house of God built, as we are the third temple (1 Pet 2:5).

Father, show me where I am sinning against You. Make me a vessel You can use to avert disaster and turn it into a house for your dwelling place, even if it costs me a lot.

Week 22, Day 6: Being the answer

He made Him who knew no sin to be sin in our behalf, so that we might become the righteousness of God in Him. 2 Corinthians 5:21

As Rees Howells grew in his understanding of intercession, God began by giving him one person to pray for, then a village and finally he was interceding for his nation during WWII. As he prayed through for one sick person, he gained authority to pray for all sick people who had that same disease. In the process, if that person had a need (e.g. for medicine), he had to pay for it himself. It was a matter of absolute obedience and being willing to be the answer to his prayers, whatever the cost. At one time, he had to be willing to die in place of a sick person, but in the end, God did not require that of him. He had to intercede until the one he was to pray for came to salvation, even if it took years. Victory comes by abiding in Christ.

When I went to live in Israel for a season, God put it on the heart of an intercessor, whom I did not even know at the time, to pray for me. For three and a half years she faithfully prayed. When I visited her, she showed me her *tallit* (prayer shawl) where she had embroidered my name. She put that *tallit* on each morning and sat before the Lord, asking Him how to pray for me that day! That is commitment. What a blessing!

When we are buried with Jesus in the waters of baptism and rise again with Him, we receive His life, which we are then to lay down in order to see others also come into the Kingdom.

Dear Lord, do a work in my heart so I become the answer to my prayers where possible.

Week 22, Day 7: The ministry of reconciliation

Now all these things are from God, who reconciled us to Himself through Christ and gave us the ministry of reconciliation...Therefore, we are ambassadors for Christ, as though God were making an appeal through us; we beg you on behalf of Christ, be reconcilied to God. 2 Corinthians 5:18, 20

The things that annoy us about other people are usually the things in ourselves, to which we are generally blind (Matt 7:3-5). God has to deal with what is in us before He will deal with others. This is what God does as we intercede for others.

Jesus did all the hard work of reconciling us to God, but He gave us the ministry of reconciliation also. An ambassador is an authorised person appointed to represent their home country in a foreign land. We are to represent the Kingdom of heaven on earth, as the Lord's ambassadors, in our temporary home here. Others are watching our lives, so we have to be good examples and walk in the light.

Intercessors are bridge builders and peacemakers. We need to be appealing to others to be reconciled with God. We only have one lifetime to make our decision as to where we will spend eternity, and that is the most important decision of our entire life (Heb 9:27).

Parents need to be intercessors for their children, godparents for their godchild, and all of us for those God calls us to stand in the gap for at any given time.

Father, teach me to be a bridge builder and peacemaker for You and take me deeper into the ministry of intercession so that I can be more effective in prayer for my family, the sick and hurting, the lost and for my country.

Week 23

The priestly role of prayer

Week 23, Day 1: A kingdom of priests

But you are a chosen people, a royal priesthood, a holy nation, God's special possession, that you may declare the praises of him who called you out of darkness into his wonderful light. 1 Peter 2:9 (NIV)

God's original plan was always to have a nation as His priesthood (Ex 19:5-6), but when Israel broke the covenant by worshipping the golden calf, Moses called for those who were for the Lord to come to him (Ex 32:26). The tribe of Levi responded, so became God's representatives to stand between His holiness and the sin of the people. Their first job was to deal with the idolaters by killing 3,000 of their brethren! That was reversed with 3,000 being saved on the day of Pentecost, when the law began to be written on hearts by the Holy Spirit.

As God's *ecclesia*, washed clean by His atoning blood, we are now the ones who are to take on this role within the tabernacle. Our ministry is to God first, then to the people (Num 16:9). We are also to represent the people to God as intercessors. There were daily morning and evening offerings in the temple on behalf of the nation as well as offering the individual sacrifices brought by the people. It was a duty for which one had to be set apart and sanctified to perform.

He appointed some of the Levites as ministers before the ark of the LORD, *to celebrate and to thank and praise the* LORD *God of Israel.* 1 Chron 16:4

Father, I ask You to set me apart that I can be a faithful priest in your service, ministering to You and the people around me.

Week 23, Day 2: Authority to bless

Then the LORD *spoke to Moses, saying, 'Speak to Aaron and to his sons, saying, "In this way you shall bless the sons of Israel. You are to say to them: The* LORD *bless you, and keep you; The* LORD *cause His face to shine on you, and be gracious to you; The* LORD *lift up His face to you, and give you peace." So they shall invoke My name on the sons of Israel, and then I will bless them.'* Numbers 6:22-27

The priests were endowed with the authority to speak blessing over the people. It is not our task to judge others – we must leave that responsibility to God as the One who sees justly (Matt 7:1-2). A blessing is not just nice words; the priestly blessing is like spreading a prayer shawl over the people to gather them together under the wings of the Lord as a community. He is their shelter and refuge in the day of trouble and His own possession (Ps 135:4). It is placing the people into God's good hands so that He can bless them, the result of which is peace. *Shalom* in Hebrew is far more than just the absence of war. It is completeness and rest, when all debts are paid, and includes prosperity, physical and emotional well-being. God wants to bless us and He also wants us to bless others. By praying for and lifting others to the Lord, as well as giving gifts or time and friendship, we can bless others and ask God to bless them, since He alone is the source of all blessing.

Pray blessing over your family and over someone who is difficult to love today. See how God works in that situation.

Week 23, Day 3: Servants

Then you shall put them [holy garments] on Aaron your brother and on his sons with him; and you shall anoint them and ordain them and consecrate them, so that they may serve Me as priests. Exodus 28:41

Priests did not choose their profession. They were chosen by God, clothed, anointed, ordained and consecrated to serve Him as priests. They were set apart for God with no other duties, and were given no land as an inheritance, only cities within the other tribes, as the Lord was their possession (Josh 13:33).

They were to be given a portion of the tithes for their food. It was their duty to teach the Law to the people. They were the spiritual keepers of the nation, responsible for the spiritual state of the nation, and were also the judges in disputes. Where there is no knowledge of God's laws or the people choose to disobey His laws, then the nation falls headlong into the outworkings of the curses – judgement, with the resultant poverty, decline, lack of productivity, disasters and chaos (Dt 28:15-68).

My people are destroyed for lack of knowledge. Since you have rejected knowledge, I also will reject you from being My priest. Since you have forgotten the Law of your God, I also will forget your children. Hos 4:6

The Western world is in this place now. God's judgements are meant to bring correction and redemption, not wrath. He raises up prophets and leaders to warn, but it is chiefly the role of the priests to keep and teach God's laws.

Father, make me faithful to live and teach your laws and your ways to my children and friends in a loving and gentle way, so they can be blessed.

Week 23, Day 4: The golden altar

Another angel came and stood at the altar, holding a golden censer; and much incense was given to him, so that he might add it to the prayers of all the saints on the golden altar which was before the throne. And the smoke of the incense ascended from the angel's hand with the prayers of the saints before God. Revelation 8:3-4

The altar of incense in the earthly tabernacle was placed immediately before the ark of the covenant, separated by the veil, and the bowls of incense were burnt upon it, forming a smoke that filled the room. The earthly temple was a pattern of the heavenly one. In the heavenly tabernacle, our prayers form the incense that rises before the throne of God. Like the High Priest on earth came before the ark on the Day of Atonement, the elders now present the petitions of the earthly redeemed priesthood to Jesus, our High Priest who brings them to the Father.

When these prayers align with heaven's will and timing and the bowls are full, they are poured out onto the earth as heavenly decrees. This is so powerful that we need to stop and absorb the immensity of it. What a privilege! We are priests ministering between heaven and earth and being part of the process of answering the prayer Jesus taught us to pray – '*Your Kingdom come on earth as it is in Heaven.*'

Meditate today on Revelation chapter 8. Ask the Lord to make this alive for you.

Week 23, Day 5: Fire on the altar

Then the angel took the censer and filled it with the fire of the altar, and hurled it to the earth; and there were peals of thunder and sounds, and flashes of lightning and an earthquake. And the seven angels who had the seven trumpets prepared themselves to sound them. Revelation 8:5-6

The role of the priests is strategic to the end-time battle. We are to be participants with the angelic forces, not just onlookers. The angel responds to the incense, adds fire from the altar then throws it to the earth. Heaven is answering the prayers and the angels are waiting to respond! Our priestly prayers stir an angelic response and angels sound the trumpets.

Since the return of the Jews to their land from around 1880, the sound of the *shofar* (horn) is again being heard across Israel. Furthermore, in prophetic circles, the *shofar* is also being blown throughout the earth. The *shofar* was used to call the people to assemble, give marching orders, warn of danger, announce holy days and the new month, year and jubilee, induct kings, bring down the walls of Jericho and welcome the coming of the Messiah. Its haunting sound is a wake-up call for us to prepare ourselves to meet our Bridegroom (Matt 25:1-13, 1 Cor 15:51-53).

For the Lord Himself will descend from heaven with a shout, with the voice of the archangel and with the trumpet of God, and the dead in Christ will rise first. Then we who are alive, who remain, will be caught up together with them in the clouds to meet the Lord in the air, and so we will always be with the Lord. 1 Thess 4:16-17

Father, show me how I can be a participant in preparing for your return, not just an onlooker.

Week 23, Day 6: Raise the standard

My covenant with him [Levi] was one of life and peace, and I gave them to him as an object of reverence; so he revered Me and was in awe of My name. True instruction was in his mouth and injustice was not found on his lips; he walked with Me in peace and justice, and he turned many back from wrongdoing. For the lips of a priest should maintain knowledge, and people should seek instruction from his mouth; for he is the messenger of the LORD of armies. Malachi 2:5-7

Malachi describes the priesthood as it should be functioning. The following verses sadly describe how they had fallen away and were not practising nor teaching holiness but offering defiled sacrifices and robbing God of tithes. When priests are corrupt the whole society falls apart. If there are repeated problems in a church (e.g. in marriages), look at what is happening in the leadership in that area. If we don't like what our government is doing, then check what is happening in the church. We are meant to set the moral standard for society, not follow the ways of the world. If we are no different, then we are not salt and light. Don't blame the unbelievers for the problems; look at the priesthood. Reform starts with the *ecclesia* weeping between the porch and the altar (Joel 2:17).

Thankfully, God says that He will send His messenger to purify the Levites and refine them like gold, but it will be by fire. Indeed, who can endure the day of His coming (Mal 3:1-3)?

Dear Lord, please make me quick to repent and keep me pure and clean so that I can minister in your temple and enter your presence. Ps 24:3-6

Week 23, Day 7: The Zadok priesthood

But the Levites who went far from Me when Israel went astray, who went astray from Me after their idols, shall bear the punishment for their iniquity...But the Levitical priests, the sons of Zadok, who took responsibility for My sanctuary when the sons of Israel went astray from Me, shall come near to Me to serve Me. Ezekiel 44:10, 15a

There is a true and a false priesthood. Ezekiel was writing about the same time as Malachi. The punishment for the false Levitical priesthood was not that they were stripped of their duties, but that they could no longer come near to God! They could minister to people only. Only the sons of Zadok were allowed to come close to God and minister in His presence. How awful to continue doing all the worldly duties of service, but all without the presence or power of God!

This is where so much of the church is today – doing good deeds that are acceptable in the eyes of the world, but lacking the commitment, power and courage to discern right from wrong, walk in holiness and teach the people the difference between the holy and the profane in God's sight (Ezek 44:23). The Zadok priests were the worshippers in the inner court, seeking His face. The Lord was their inheritance and they were His possession, blessed with the first fruits offering for themselves and their household (v.28-30).

God is calling us to dare to be different: to forget about fame, reputation, ambition, wealth and all the lures of the world, and to come into His presence and minister to Him. Are you willing?

Lord, make me willing to sacrifice all to You, no matter what everyone around me is doing. Let me rejoice in the unseen ministry that brings pleasure to You alone.

The Many Facets of Prayer

Week 24
Prayers of blessing

Week 24, Day 1: The power of blessing

Bless the LORD, my soul, and all that is within me, bless His holy name. Bless the LORD, my soul, and do not forget any of His benefits. Psalm 103:1-2

Blessing is powerful. The Hebrew *barak* means to kneel or bless, which is to endue with power for success, prosperity, fertility and longevity. Who does not want that? God is the source of blessing and the only One who has the power to give abundant life. It is God's desire, because of His loving nature, to want to bless all His creation. Psalm 103 goes on to thank God for the blessings He has given us – forgiveness, healing, redemption, favour, compassion, provision and strength. That is a very good place to start. We bless God by being thankful for the blessings He has given us. We bless others by sharing those blessings in word and deed.

It was a priestly duty to bless, first of all, God, then also the people (Num 6:22-27). The nature of the blessing was to put the name of the Lord over the people. They were to be His chosen people under His wings of protection with His face shining on them. In the same way, the Lord is watching over us who bear His name, wanting to bless us, and through us our families, friends, communities and nations. As we reach out to bless in His name, we are partnering with Him to bring redemption to our broken world.

Dear Lord, show me who I am to bless today and each day and how You would have me do this. Make me a blessing to others I pray.

Week 24, Day 2: The gift of encouragement

Therefore, encourage one another and build one another up, just as you also are doing. 1 Thessalonians 5:11

The gift of encouragement releases hope, faith and love. I was blessed to have a pastor for many years who had this gift and exercised it daily. Each day she would ask the Lord who she could encourage that day. She would then write little notes and post them off or pick up the phone to express her gratitude. As a teacher, she was always speaking words of praise over her students. From the pulpit, she told stories that built everyone's faith. When in hospital, she encouraged her fellow patients as she saw endurance, courage or progress and brought joy to the staff as she never complained but expressed her thanks for their service. It was a joy to be with her and the love of God shone forth from her, bringing life and hope to the discouraged.

Flattery is buttering someone up in the hope of gaining favour. Encouragement is expressed from a genuine heart of love, which breaks down barriers of resistance and causes people to open their hearts to God and others. It builds the recipients up, and people then gain confidence to be their true self rather than feeling they need to wear masks to be accepted. It is a fantastic tool for evangelism.

We can ask God to give us this precious gift but also work to cultivate this attitude of gratitude and see the potential in people as God sees them. If we follow this up with prayer and call people into their destiny in God through the good gifts He has endowed them with, we will see them emerge from their cocoons and transform into the butterflies God has created them to be.

Precious Lord, please give me this gift and turn me into a butterfly breeder!

Week 24, Day 3: The Sabbath blessing

By the seventh day God completed His work which He had done, and He rested on the seventh day from all His work which He had done. Then God blessed the seventh day and sanctified it, because on it He rested from all His work which God had created and made. Genesis 2:2-3

I have heard many Jews say that the Sabbath has kept them, rather than them keeping the Sabbath. This precious time, instituted by God from sunset on Friday to sundown on Saturday, has kept Jewish families together for four thousand years. Not only did God take time to rest and enjoy His creation, but having created human beings on the sixth day, their first day on earth was to be one of taking time to enjoy the presence of God and one another. Work came later.

In our busy world, packed with a thousand things to do, we need to take time to rest and enjoy life and God's creation. The Jewish Sabbath begins with setting the time apart for prayers, for a family meal and spending time together. Attending the synagogue follows the next morning. The Friday night prayers include the father blessing his wife with Proverbs 31:10-31, thus being thankful and praising her attributes. After this, the father individually lays hands on each of the children and blesses them in the same way. I have personally experienced this in Jewish families, and it is so powerful. Oh, how the church needs to restore this precious practice. God blessed time and sanctified it before anything else. We need to do the same.

Father, help me to set apart time to rest in You and to restore the Father's blessing by investing time with my family.

Week 24, Day 4: Encouraging the body

Let's consider how to encourage one another in love and good deeds, not abandoning our own meeting together, as is the habit of some people, but encouraging one another; and all the more as you see the day drawing near. Hebrews 10:24-25

As a teacher or as a parent, we need to remember that the proportion of our efforts need to be 70% encouragement and 30% correction. It is very easy to see the faults that glare at us and clamour for attention, but we often forget that we all respond much better to correction when it is cushioned in the acknowledgement of our good characteristics. When we know we are loved by the other person, we will welcome the fact that they want to keep us on track. Unconditional acceptance is a prerequisite for correction to be taken on board.

The Scriptures exhort us to keep meeting together as the body of Christ and to encourage one another (1 Thess 5:11). The tougher life gets, the more we need to band together and build one another up. It is easy these days to send an encouraging text or link to a worship song. It is even more effective to meet and encourage someone personally. When we take time to ask the Lord for an encouraging word for someone else, then He will surely answer that, as it reflects His heart. Encouraging one another into holiness is far more important than happiness. As a young adult, some friends and I agreed together to ask, 'How are you growing (in God)', rather than 'How are you going'? This gives accountability and a call to holy living, which we should all seek, rather than just the pursuit of happiness.

Am I being accountable in my life? Do I need to find a spiritual mentor or life coach?

Week 24, Day 5: Prayers of blessing

So, as those who have been chosen of God, holy and beloved, put on a heart of compassion, kindness, humility, gentleness, and patience; bearing with one another, and forgiving each other, whoever has a complaint against anyone; just as the Lord forgave you, so must you do also. In addition to all these things put on love, which is the perfect bond of unity. Colossians 3:12-14

It is not hard to bless those we love and cherish, with whom we are in agreement and share one heart. It is quite another to release blessing to the people we find hard to love. Yet this is a powerful weapon. Seeking to bless forces us to look for the good in the other person. It seeks their good and not their demise! It wants their prosperity and success, not their failure. As we focus on this and ask the Lord for His good plans for those who may be persecuting us or wanting to remove us, our mindset has to change. When we begin to see the person as a child of God, loved by Him and for whom He gave His life, we begin to love even the unlovable.

With it [our tongue] we bless our Lord and Father, and with it we curse people, who have been made in the likeness of God; from the same mouth come both blessing and cursing. My brothers and sisters, these things should not be this way. James 3:9-10

There is life and death in the power of the tongue (Prov 18:21). Our tongue can deliver blessing or deadly poison (Jas 3:8). Our words need to be ones of blessing, not cursing. As we cultivate and pray prayers of blessing for our enemies or the unsaved, our hearts will come into alignment with the heart of God. We can then release genuine words of blessing to them.

Dear Lord, teach me to pray prayers of blessing and to temper my words to build others up, not pull them down.

Week 24, Day 6: The language of love

We have different gifts, according to the grace given to each of us. If your gift is prophesying, then prophesy in accordance with your faith; if it is serving, then serve; if it is teaching, then teach; if it is to encourage, then give encouragement; if it is giving, then give generously; if it is to lead, do it diligently; if it is to show mercy, do it cheerfully. Romans 12:6-8 (NIV)

Marriage counsellor, Gary Chapman, wrote his bestselling book, *The Five Languages of Love*.[1] The first of these languages is the giving of compliments or words of affirmation. This applies not only to marriage but to any relationship. Affirming children gives them confidence in their abilities and assurance of love. It gives them courage to step out and develop and use their gifts. We all need this, especially in our developmental years or early stages of trying something new. It is easy to give up and lose heart if we do not have this encouragement.

Encouragement is even more precious when we have just messed something up. We are then prone to self-condemnation and feel like a failure. If someone then comes with a word of encouragement or comes alongside to help repair our mess, it is an act of selflessness that shows the heart of God. Those who are depressed, have lost hope or are desperate, especially need this ministry. There are many on our streets who fit this category, and God loves them all.

Dear Jesus, help me to be one to come alongside the downtrodden and hopeless ones to lift their heads and their hearts to see your nature.

Week 24, Day 7: Building one another up

Let the message of Christ dwell among you richly as you teach and admonish one another with all wisdom through psalms, hymns, and songs from the Spirit, singing to God with gratitude in your hearts. Colossians 3:16 (NIV)

As we abide in Christ and His Word lives in us, this treasure will begin to flow out through us as living water. An Australian evangelist I know is a wonderful example of this. She is not young and has multiple serious health challenges. In fact, at her age, most of us would have retired, put our feet up and only be looking to enjoy the rest of our lives in as much comfort as possible. Not this lady. She is on a mission in a country where the word 'missionary' is a dirty word. She does not run a ministry, she has no large organisation providing her finances, but she faces each new day with the joy of the Lord. As she goes about her daily life, she takes this joy with her and sets out to bless everyone with whom she has contact. She trusts in God's provision, giving finance or gifts if she feels that is needed, despite not having a lot of her own. She asks if she can pray for those suffering oppression or despondency. She gives words of encouragement to everyone she meets. She just follows the Lord's leading to bless people in any way she can, and God honours that with many coming to know the Lord.

This lady is doing what all of us can do, but most of us don't. The blessing is not meant to just be for us to enjoy. It is meant for us to pass on to the lost world. Whether it is our neighbour, the local shopkeeper, the doctor, the mechanic or the plumber, we are all interacting with someone who needs to be blessed and know the God of love.

Abba Father, teach me to bless others as You bless me.

The Many Facets of Prayer

Week 25
Evangelism and prayer

Week 25, Day 1: In season and out of season

Preach the word; be ready in season and out of season; correct, rebuke, and exhort, with great patience and instruction. For the time will come when they will not tolerate sound doctrine; but wanting to have their ears tickled, they will accumulate for themselves teachers in accordance with their own desires, and they will turn their ears away from the truth and will turn aside to myths. 2 Timothy 4:2-4

Paul tells us that we are all gifted in something but not all are gifted in preaching or teaching or evangelism. However, we must all be ready to speak about Jesus when we have an opportunity. Praying for those opportunities will mean that they come more often. We have to take the good news to the world, not expect the world to come to us. Outgoing personalities find it easier to approach strangers than introverts, but a smile and a compliment can open many doors. We can learn from those who are gifted and also improve with teaching and knowing how to access resources that are available.

Your testimony is one of the most effective tools for evangelism. No one can deny what you have personally experienced. Share your story, then ask if the person can identify with any part of what you have shared. If so, take it from there; if not, move on to others.

Dear Lord, I ask You to give me opportunities to share my story with others. Open doors that no man can shut.

Week 25, Day 2: If I am lifted up

And I, if I am lifted up from the earth, will draw all people to Myself. John 12:32

I heard a story of George Mueller (I think) who was preaching on the street in London and being hassled by some rowdy hecklers who were mocking God. He stopped speaking and listened to them for a while. As the crowd clapped the ringleader, Mueller joined them. Caught by surprise, they asked why *he* was applauding. He replied that the sort of god they were describing was not worthy of honour. Having got their attention, he then went on to tell them about the true character of the God he served – and of course, many then accepted the Lord.

Sing praises to the LORD, who dwells in Zion; declare His deeds among the peoples. Ps 9:11

When we lift Jesus up, then He will draw all men to Himself. When we exalt Him, we are declaring His glory to the world. We declare His awesome deeds, His mighty works, His Word, His wonders, His creation, His justice, His righteousness, and His faithfulness. People need to see God at work now, not just on the pages of an ancient book. Jesus always demonstrated His power, compassion or healing and then asked people to follow Him, not the reverse. There is nothing like a supernatural healing or an accurate word of knowledge to get someone's attention. We must believe and pray for these signs and wonders that accompany the preaching of the gospel (Mk 16:15-18). The power of the gospel is in the cross and resurrection of Jesus, not our ability to convince others. He is glorified far more in our weakness than in our strength.

For I determined to know nothing among you except Jesus Christ, and Him crucified. 1 Cor 2:2

Abba Father, I give You my weakness to use to show your glory and draw people to You.

Week 25, Day 3: Work of the Spirit

I will send Him [the Helper/the Holy Spirit] *to you. And He, when He comes, will convict the world regarding sin, and righteousness, and judgment:* John 16:7e-8

We are called to love the unbeliever unconditionally as Jesus does, not to judge or condemn them (Jn 13:34-35). As we do this, the Holy Spirit can work to bring conviction. When people are excited about Jesus and bubble over with enthusiasm, it is infectious, and many catch it! The best evangelists I know have a gift of perceiving the need of others, especially their emotional need, and ministering to that deep place that we do not easily expose, but when it is uncovered, there is a release and the seeds of the gospel take root. They never tell people what they should believe, but invite them to consider Jesus and meet Him.

In generations past, when the Ten Commandments were taught in schools, displayed in law courts and the Lord's Prayer recited daily in parliament, people had a sense of what God required of us. Now, a vast majority of the population are ignorant. The knowledge of sin has disappeared in a society that is taught 'if it feels good, do it'. Despite this, most people would not claim to be perfect; they just believe they are not bad enough to deserve hell, so can earn their way to heaven. People must see their need for Christ and that He is the only one who can meet that need. We need to help them understand that 'the wages of sin is death' (Rom 6:23). Repentance is an essential part of salvation, without which there is no true conversion.

Lord, I pray for the reinstatement of basic biblical teaching like the Ten Commandments and the Sermon on the Mount in schools and universities so there is a restoration of the knowledge of sin, right and wrong, good and evil as You see it. Jn 3:16, 2 Pet 3:9

Week 25, Day 4: Word and deed

For our gospel did not come to you in word only, but also in power and in the Holy Spirit and with full conviction; just as you know what kind of men we proved to be among you for your sakes. 1 Thessalonians 1:5

It is vitally important that our lives match what we are preaching. We must live the Word, not just preach the Word. Paul was able to say 'do as I do'; 'imitate me' (1 Cor 11:1). Our lives are our witness. We are living letters that will be read by all those around us (2 Cor 3:2-3). Paul says we are not saved by our works, but they are the evidence of the gospel working in our lives whereas James tells us that words without deeds are empty (James 2:17-18). James and Paul are not in conflict; we need both word and deed, not one without the other. There are many doing humanitarian work, but without preaching the gospel, it is simply human kindness.

For we are His workmanship, created in Christ Jesus for good works, which God prepared beforehand so that we would walk in them. Eph 2:10

Your light must shine before people in such a way that they may see your good works, and glorify your Father who is in heaven. Matt 5:16

Father, show me the good works You have for me to do. Let me walk in them. May my light shine consistently in both word and deed.

Week 25, Day 5: Athens

Paul stood in the midst of the Areopagus and said, 'Men of Athens, I see that you are very religious in all respects. For while I was passing through and examining the objects of your worship, I also found an altar with this inscription, "To an unknown god." Therefore, what you worship in ignorance, this I proclaim to you.' Acts 17:22-23

When Paul came to Athens, he first observed the city, which he found full of idols. He then reasoned with the Jews in the synagogue and with the philosophers in the marketplace. When invited, he gave a speech to the city councillors. He began with a compliment and spoke of what he had observed about their gods, picking up on the 'unknown god' they worshipped without knowledge, then explained to them the gospel. While some responded, many ridiculed. There were not enough believers to begin a church at that time, though this followed later. The Greek spirit of unbelief that hardened their hearts still rules over our culture today.

In my experience, trying to argue about the Bible with people is one of the least effective ways to evangelise. We do need to be able to give a reasoned response for why we believe, but the gospel is sown into soft hearts, not hard heads!

Lord, I pray for a softening of the hearts of those I know who need salvation. Take out the hearts of stone and replace them with a heart of flesh. Ezek 36:27-28

Week 25, Day 6: Corinth

My message and my preaching were not in persuasive words of wisdom, but in demonstration of the Spirit and of power, so that your faith would not rest on the wisdom of mankind, but on the power of God. 1 Corinthians 2:4-5

Paul went from Athens on to Corinth. Corinth was a renowned city of sin. Through the narrow isthmus near Corinth, boats were hauled overland in order to save the long journey around the headland. The sailors disembarked and revelled in the licentious behaviour that lured them to Corinth. Despite this, Paul had a very long and effective ministry there. He stayed about 18 months. His success there was not due to debate or human wisdom, but by focussing on the power of the cross and demonstration of God's power to change and reform lives.

Well-educated, well-paid citizens are generally not the most open to the gospel. Jesus went to the highways and byways to fill the places for the wedding feast (Matt 22:9). The down-and-outs are those who most see their need. Are we willing to go to those broken ones and give them a hand and show them the way back to the light? By humbling ourselves to do so, we may be welcoming angels unaware (Heb 13:2). They will have the best testimonies once they are saved. No one is too lost that Jesus cannot redeem. Will we pass by on the other side, or will we be the good Samaritan (Lk 10:30-37)?

Lord, I pray for the restoration of signs and wonders and the return to the preaching of the true gospel focussing on the cross and resurrection of Jesus, not tickling people's ears.

Week 25, Day 7: Revive us

For though I am free from all people, I have made myself a slave to all, so that I may gain more. To the Jews I became as a Jew, so that I might gain Jews... To the weak I became weak, that I might gain the weak; I have become all things to all people, so that I may by all means save some. 1 Corinthians 9:19-20a, 22

Paul was willing to lay aside his learning, his pride, all earthly ambitions and comforts in order to save some. Nothing happens in God's Kingdom without being birthed in sacrifice and prayer. If we want to see revival and reformation, we have to count the cost.

In 1898, a petition with 15,300 signatures was sent to D.L.Moody in the US asking him to come and lead a crusade in Australia. He died before he could come, but in 1902, R.A.Torrey came and led a crusade in Melbourne. With the population of Melbourne then 500,000, over 250,000 people came every week! Ten thousand *men* filled the Exhibition Building to pray. Over 8,500 people came to Christ during the crusades![1]

It all began when a dozen or so men began to pray each week for revival and did so for years. Before Torrey arrived, there were 1,700 neighbourhood prayer meetings being held every week, praying for an outpouring of the Spirit. They had organised the city into 50 sections, and each had their own preparatory meeting. Every home was visited twice before the outreach. That is commitment that God answers.

Oh, dear Lord, do it again in our day.

The Many Facets of Prayer

Week 26
Angels and prayer

Week 26, Day 1: Good and bad angels

The angel of the LORD encamps around those who fear Him, and rescues them. Psalm 34:7

There are 287 references to angels in the Bible, 176 of them in the New Testament, so this is not a topic we should discount or ignore. Angels are God's heavenly messengers and agents to carry out His divine will. Interestingly, the first reference is when the angel appeared to Sarah's maid, Hagar, a Gentile Egyptian, giving a direct prophecy concerning Ishmael (Gen 16:7-12)!

Angels fall into several categories: cherubim are archangels (living creatures that surround the throne of God), seraphim (burning ones), and teraphim (watchers). These latter ones can take on human form. In Jewish thought, there were originally six cherubim – Michael, Gabriel, Raphael, Uriel, Lucifer (Satan) and Abaddon. The last two fell and it is believed they took a third of the angels with them (Ezek 28:13-19, Is 14:9-15, Rev 9:11, 12:3-4 and the book of Enoch). A devil is a fallen angel or 'evil spirit', the Nephilim (Gen 6:4) are the offspring of teraphim and humans, and demons are disembodied souls of dead Nephilim, or 'unclean spirits.'[1] The book of Enoch was well known in New Testament times and is referred to in the books of Jude, 1 and 2 Peter. Jesus also accepted that there were angels in heaven (Matt 22:30) and the devil and his angels (Matt 25:41).

The spiritual realm is as real today as it was in Jesus' time and before. We need our spiritual eyes and ears open to see and hear what is happening in the heavenlies.

Thank You, Lord, that You have already won the war over the demonic forces.

Week 26, Day 2: Worshipping angels

Then I looked and heard the voice of many angels, numbering thousands upon thousands, and ten thousand times ten thousand. They encircled the throne and the living creatures and the elders. In a loud voice they were saying: 'Worthy is the Lamb, who was slain, to receive power and wealth and wisdom and strength and honour and glory and praise!' Revelation 5:11-12 (NIVUK)

Angels are eternal beings. We do not become angels after we go to heaven. In the book of Revelation, we catch a glimpse of the worship that is happening around the throne of God. A major part of the angels' service is in worship to the Father. They extol the attributes of His character – holiness, worthiness, power, wisdom, glory etc. The four living creatures and the twenty-four elders hold the bowls of incense which are the prayers of the saints. The worship and the prayers activate the unfolding of the events that cause judgement on the earth to purify it and make it ready for the Lamb to receive His earthly inheritance.

It is the angels that carry out the work and purposes of God – the seals, the trumpets, the bowls of wrath and the declarations of Revelation 14:6-20. They also watch over the seven churches in chapters 1-3 represented as stars (Rev 1:16, 20). But when they are not sent on assignment, they are in heaven worshipping the Lord. There are innumerable angels around the throne at the Lord's disposal and they are happy when we join with them offering up prayers in alignment with God's heart so they can present them to the Lord and go forth to fulfil them.

Lord God, show me how to join with the worship of heaven in unison with the worshippers.

Week 26, Day 3: Warrior angels

I shall now return to fight against the prince of Persia; so I am leaving, and behold, the prince of Greece is about to come. However, I will tell you what is recorded in the writing of truth. Yet there is no one who stands firmly with me against these forces except Michael your prince. Daniel 10:20b-21

One of God's names is the Lord of Hosts – literally, the Lord of the armies of heaven. He is a warrior King (Ex 15:3, Zeph 3:17) and when He returns, He will come to war against His enemies (Rev 19:11). The Lord's army is the host of angelic warrior angels. We are no doubt more familiar and comfortable with God as a loving, kind and merciful God, but He can also be a God of war (Ps 3:7, 68:1).

Michael is an appointed warrior archangel on behalf of Israel against the dragon (the serpent, Satan) and his cohorts (Dan 10:13,21, 12:1, Rev 12:7-9). The battle is ultimately spiritual but can have physical consequences as well. Israel had to fight when they first entered the land, and also now since their return from the ends of the earth. Satan opposes anything to do with God and will fight to keep people from accepting the Lord, getting closer to Him or following Him as individuals or as nations. Most of all, he will try, at all cost, to stop the return of Jesus to take up His throne on Mt Zion – and that ultimately explains the battle in the Middle East.

Angels can execute the judgement of God, as against Sodom and Gomorrah (Gen 19:1,13), the Assyrian army (2 Kgs 19:35), Herod (Acts 12:20-23) and in the book of Revelation.

Thank You Father for the heavenly host of angels that are fighting on my behalf to protect me and all your children and carry out your will on earth.

Week 26, Day 4: Guardian angels

Behold, I am going to send an angel before you to guard you along the way and to bring you into the place which I have prepared. Be attentive to him and obey his voice...since My name is in him. Exodus 23:20-21

Israel was promised a guardian angel who would lead them through the desert and protect them as a cloud by day and a fire by night. There is no scriptural proof for the common idea of a personal guardian angel assigned to us, but in the lovely psalm of protection we read:

For He will give His angels orders concerning you, to protect you in all your ways. On their hands they will lift you up, so that you do not strike your foot against a stone. Ps 91:11-12

Cherubim are the guardians around the heavenly throne. The ark on earth, patterned after the heavenly reality, was also guarded by two cherubim (Ex 25:18-22). The curtains were to be embroidered with cherubim (Ex 26:1). Cherubim also guarded the way back to the tree of life after Adam and Eve were cast out of the garden of Eden (Gen 3:24).

The Holy Spirit is now our guide, but this does not discount the possibility of God sending angels to look after us, especially in times of danger. I have heard many stories of angels or 'people' appearing at strategic times of need, assisting in the situation, then suddenly vanishing. Be prepared for God's suddenlies!

Thank You, Abba, for always being there when I call upon You and guarding my going out and my coming in. Ps 121:8

Week 26, Day 5: Messenger angels

But the angel said to her, 'Do not be afraid, Mary, you have found favour with God. You will conceive and give birth to a son, and you are to call him Jesus. He will be great and will be called the Son of the Most High. The Lord God will give him the throne of his father David, and he will reign over Jacob's descendants for ever; his kingdom will never end.' Luke 1:30-33 (NIVUK)

Most often in the Scriptures, when angels appear on earth, it is to bring a message. That message may be a warning of something about to happen (Gen 19:1, 13; Matt 2:13), an announcement of what God wanted the person to do (Gen 16:9, Lk 1:11-15) or to guide through unfamiliar waters (Gen 24:40). 'Angel' in Hebrew means 'messenger'. In some cases, in the Old Testament, the messengers are understood to be pre-incarnations of Jesus. Sometimes they appear in dreams (to Jacob in Gen 28:12, to Joseph in Matt 1:20,) or in visions (to Cornelius in Acts 10:3), and at other times as a person (to Moses in Ex 3:2, to Peter in Acts 5:19, 12:7). Notice that angels did not cease to appear with the outpouring of the Holy Spirit but continued to guide the early apostles.

And behold, an angel of the Lord suddenly stood near Peter, and a light shone in the cell; and he struck Peter's side and woke him, saying, 'Get up quickly.' And his chains fell off his hands. And the angel said to him, 'Put on your belt and strap on your sandals.' And he did so. And he said to him, 'Wrap your cloak around you and follow me.' Acts 12:7-8

Father, I thank You that You have hosts of angels at your disposal to answer our prayers and guide us. What You did for the apostles You can still do today.

Week 26, Day 6: Ministering angels

Are they not all ministering spirits, sent out to provide service for the sake of those who will inherit salvation? Hebrews 1:14

An angel met Hagar in the desert after Sarah had sent her away. He gave her direction to return and gave her hope and a future for the son she was carrying (Gen 16:7-14). An angel also came to strengthen Elijah after he had fled from Ahab and Jezebel (1 Kgs 19:5-8).

When Jesus was agonising over his upcoming death and praying for the disciples, His Father sent angels to minister to Him and strengthen Him (Lk 22:42-43). They also rolled away the stone on Jesus' grave (Matt 28:2) and comforted the women after the resurrection, announcing that Jesus had risen from the dead (Lk 24:4-7).

It is the angels that collect our prayers and bring them before the throne of God (Rev 5:8). What a wonderful picture! They are no doubt seeking to have more to collect to fill their bowls of incense to the brim so the Lord can send them out to answer those prayers.

Another angel came and stood at the altar, holding a golden censer; and much incense was given to him, so that he might add it to the prayers of all the saints of the golden altar which was before the throne. And the smoke of the incense ascended from the angle's hand with the prayer of the saints before God. Rev 8:3-4

Thank You, Lord, for the ministering angels. May I fill up the bowls with my prayers and keep your angels busy. Ps 103:20-21

Week 26, Day 7: Worship the Lord

Do not let anyone who delights in false humility and the worship of angels disqualify you. Such a person also goes into great detail about what they have seen; they are puffed up with idle notions by their unspiritual mind. They have lost connection with the head, from whom the whole body, supported and held together by its ligaments and sinews, grows as God causes it to grow. Colossians 2:18-19 (NIVUK)

Angels are not to be worshipped. We need to be very careful with any revelation that God gives us, as it is easy to let spiritual pride creep in and then we can spoil something beautiful by speaking about it presumptuously, to the wrong people or before God's time. If we are blessed with an angelic visitation or messenger from the Lord, we need to take heed of what was said to John:

I, John, am the one who heard and saw these things. And when I heard and saw them, I fell down to worship at the feet of the angel who showed me these things. And he said to me, 'Do not do that; I am a fellow servant of yours and of your brothers the prophets, and of those who keep the words of this book. Worship God!' Rev 22:8-9

The Lord God alone is worthy of our worship. Although people spoke with angels, we are never told to try to call on them or to pray to them. Jesus did not even do this when He could have done so (Matt 26:53). Angels are sent to do the Father's bidding, not ours. We are never to invoke spirits of the dead (Lev 19:31). This is witchcraft, and if you have ever engaged in this in any way, repent and seek deliverance. Remember, there are good angels and evil angels. The spiritual realm is real and is dangerous if we are in the wrong camp.

Father, forgive me for ever seeking any advice from soothsayers or any occult source. I thank You for your angelic messengers that serve You and help and guide us in truth.

The Many Facets of Prayer

Week 27

Praying like Paul

Week 27, Day 1: Prayers of thanksgiving

We always thank God for all of you and continually mention you in our prayers. We remember before our God and Father your work produced by faith, your labour prompted by love, and your endurance inspired by hope in our Lord Jesus Christ. 1 Thessalonians 1:2-3 NIVUK

Paul had a grateful heart. He begins most of his letters by expressing gratitude to God and thanking Him for the people he was writing to and assuring them that he was praying for them. He had a deep love for the congregations, and he was always thanking God for them.

His main reason for thanks was for their faith (Rom 1:8, Eph 1:15-16, 1 Thess 1:2-3, 2 Thess 1:3, 2 Tim 1:3-5, Philemon 1:4-6) and the love that they displayed for the saints and for one another (Eph 1:15, Col 1:3-4, 1 Thess 1:2-3, 2 Thess 1:3, Philemon 1:5, 7). The other thing he was grateful for was their endurance and perseverance through suffering and persecution (2 Thess 1:4-5). Are these things top on our priority list?

When writing to the Corinthians, he thanked God that they lacked no spiritual gift, even though he was writing to them about spiritual gifts (1 Cor 1:7). He was also appreciative for their generosity to supply for the needs of the saints (2 Cor 9:12). He was grateful to the Philippians for their partnership in the gospel (Phil 1:5).

Dear Lord, I thank You for those whose faith has been a blessing to me. May I express that to them to encourage them also.

Week 27, Day 2: Prayers of praise

Oh, the depth of the riches of the wisdom and knowledge of God! How unsearchable his judgments and his paths beyond tracing out! 'Who has known the mind of the Lord? Or who has been his counsellor? Who has ever given to God, that God should repay them?' For from him and through him and for him are all things. To him be the glory for ever! Amen. Romans 11:33-36 (NIVUK)

Paul broke into praise to God for His amazing and unfathomable plan to save the Gentiles by the Jews' hardness of heart (to believe in Jesus the Messiah) and then to save the Jews by making them jealous of the Gentiles' salvation (See Romans chapters 9-11)! This is definitely not a plan any human would concoct. Pray that the church would understand this mystery.

Surprisingly, Paul also praises God for His compassion and comfort to the Corinthians in their suffering because this would enable them to comfort others facing the same difficulties (2 Cor 1:3-7). Again, this is not how most of us think today!

Paul opens the letter to the Ephesians with praise to the Lord for His blessings. We are chosen to be holy and blameless, and predestined to be His children. He has given us redemption through the blood of Jesus, forgiveness for our sins by His grace, and made known the mystery of His will to bring all things together in Christ. We have an inheritance in Christ – hope and salvation, and are sealed with the Holy Spirit as a promise of our redemption, to the glory of God (Eph 1:3-14).

Lord Jesus, I lift up my praise to You for all the blessings that You have given me this day. (List as many as you can think of now and continue throughout the day).

Week 27, Day 3: Ephesians 1

[My prayers are] that the God of our Lord Jesus Christ, the Father of glory, may give you a spirit of wisdom and of revelation in the knowledge of Him. I pray that the eyes of your heart may be enlightened, so that you will know what is the hope of His calling, what are the riches of the glory of His inheritance in the saints, and what is the boundless greatness of His power toward us who believe. These are in accordance with the working of the strength of His might which He brought about in Christ, when He raised Him from the dead and seated Him at His right hand in the heavenly places, far above all rule and authority and power and dominion, and every name that is named, not only in this age but also in the one to come. And He put all things in subjection under His feet, and made Him head over all things to the church, which is His body, the fullness of Him who fills all in all. Ephesians 1:17-23

There is so much included in this amazing prayer. Paul catches a vision of the exalted Lord, raised from the dead and seated at the Father's right hand, reigning as King above all powers for eternity. Jesus is in total control and head over His *ecclesia* to whom He manifests the fullness of who He is, and through them to the world. Paul prays that the Lord would grant us wisdom and revelation to see Jesus in this way, and that our hearts and eyes would be opened to know the hope of His calling on our lives, the glorious inheritance He has bestowed on us and His resurrection power available to us.

Pray this prayer and insert your name. Pray it daily for someone who needs to know the Lord.

Week 27, Day 4: Ephesians 3

For this reason I bend my knees before the Father, from whom every family in heaven and on earth derives its name, that He would grant you, according to the riches of His glory, to be strengthened with power through His Spirit in the inner self, so that Christ may dwell in your hearts through faith; and that you, being rooted and grounded in love, may be able to comprehend with all the saints what is the width and length and height and depth, and to know the love of Christ which surpasses knowledge, that you may be filled to all the fullness of God. Now to Him who is able to do far more abundantly beyond all that we ask or think, according to the power that works within us, to Him be the glory in the church and in Christ Jesus to all generations forever and ever. Amen. Ephesians 3:14-21

In order to be filled with the fullness of God, we need to have a revelation of the vastness of the love of Christ for us. Paul says this surpasses knowledge and is not something that we can comprehend by human means, but he knows that God can do way beyond what we can imagine, through His power working in us. He asks that God would do what we can't and give us this revelation. Stop now and allow the Father to answer Paul's prayer in your life.

It is the indwelling presence of Christ in us through the power of the Holy Spirit that enables the fullness of God to fill us. When our faith is rooted and grounded in the knowledge of His love, it will automatically flow out to others. Our broken and hurting world so needs to see a demonstration of this love. Let it start in us.

Meditate today on the love of God and allow the Lord to fill you with that love.

Week 27, Day 5: Colossians, Philippians

...[We] have not ceased praying for you and asking that you may be filled with the knowledge of His will in all spiritual wisdom and understanding so that you will walk in a manner worthy of the Lord, to please Him in all respects, bearing fruit in every good work and increasing in the knowledge of God; strengthened with all power, according to His glorious might, for the attaining of all perseverance and patience; joyfully giving thanks to the Father, who has qualified us to share in the inheritance of the saints in light. Colossians 1:9-12

Paul was praying this way because the Colossians had an eternal perspective of the hope of heaven that caused them to have faith in Jesus and love for the brethren. They had been rescued from the domain of darkness into the Kingdom of the light (v.13). We can only please God and bear fruit when we have spiritual understanding and the knowledge of His will and can only have perseverance and patience when we have the knowledge of God and the strength of His power.

And this I pray, that your love may overflow still more and more in real knowledge and all discernment, so that you may discover the things that are excellent, that you may be sincere and blameless for the day of Christ; having been filled with the fruit of righteousness which comes through Jesus Christ, for the glory and praise of God. Phil 1:9-11

Paul's concerns are for greater love, knowledge of God, spiritual discernment, pursuit of the excellent, and fruit of holiness and righteousness, all of which will bring glory to God.

Dear Lord, reset the focus of my prayers so they reflect the prayers of your apostle Paul.

Week 27, Day 6: Thessalonians

With this in mind, we constantly pray for you, that our God may make you worthy of his calling, and that by his power he may bring to fruition your every desire for goodness and your every deed prompted by faith. We pray this so that the name of our Lord Jesus may be glorified in you, and you in him, according to the grace of our God and the Lord Jesus Christ. 2 Thessalonians 1:11-12 (NIVUK)

The Thessalonian church was suffering persecution. In spite of their difficulties, Paul focuses not on them being taken out of the persecution but rather holding firm to the Lord, being a faithful witness through the hard times and growing in love and holiness (1Thess 3:12-13). It reminds me of brother Yun, the Chinese pastor who endured years of incarceration for his faith, urging us in the West not to pray for the persecution to end, but rather that the backs of the prisoners would be strengthened. His main reason for this was seeing the complacency of the Western church. We need to be more concerned about one another's growth to mature love and holiness than our happiness and comfort which can lull us into apathy and a spiritual coma. 'When the going gets tough, the tough get going'. Persecution will sift the wheat from the chaff.

Paul prays for the Thessalonians for encouragement and strength in good deeds (2 Thess 2:16-17), that they may be protected from the evil one (2 Thess 3:3), and for their hearts to be directed into God's love and Christ's perseverance (2 Thess 3:5). Finally, he prays for peace (2 Thess 3:16).

Stir us up Lord to have a zeal and passion for You, and to encourage one another to love and good deeds. Heb 10:24

Week 27, Day 7: Paul's prayers for himself

Pray also for me, that whatever I speak, words may be given me so that I will fearlessly make known the mystery of the gospel, for which I am an ambassador in chains. Pray that I may declare it fearlessly, as I should. Ephesians 6:19-20 (NIVUK)

The letters of Ephesians, Philippians, Colossians and Philemon were all written while Paul was in prison, not because he had done anything wrong but for his preaching of the gospel. Yet not once does he ask others to pray that he be released! And the jails in which he was kept were not like ours today. Prisoners were kept in stocks or chained and kept on stone floors. Despite this, he was not concerned for his own comfort and was not complaining at his harsh treatment. He never prayed for persecution to end or for a lighter cross to bear. His only concern was that he would faithfully preach the gospel wherever he was, thus fulfilling His calling. He asked that hearts would be open to receive his message.

Devote yourselves to prayer, being watchful and thankful. And pray for us, too, that God may open a door for our message, so that we may proclaim the mystery of Christ, for which I am in chains. Pray that I may proclaim it clearly, as I should. Col 4:2-4 (NIVUK)

Paul did pray three times that the thorn in his flesh may be taken away, but was content when the Lord told him, '*My grace is sufficient for you, for power is perfected in weakness.*' (2 Cor 12:7-9).

Lord, forgive my complaining and seeking for the things of this world rather than the extension of your Kingdom. Give me a passion and urgency to see others saved.

Week 28
Travailing prayer

Week 28, Day 1: The price of revival

You will hear of wars and rumours of wars, but see to it that you are not alarmed. Such things must happen, but the end is still to come. Nation will rise against nation, and kingdom against kingdom. There will be famines and earthquakes in various places. All these are the beginning of birth-pains. Matthew 24:6-8 (NIVUK)

The labour pains that precede birth are said to be the most intense pain that a woman will ever experience in life. As in the natural, so in the spiritual. When we are birthing the Kingdom purposes in our life, praying for breakthrough for another or birthing revival in our nation, travail is the intense, desperate prayer that Jesus likens to birth pangs. The Spirit groans within us in a way that is too deep for words, but words are not necessary, as it is spirit-to-Spirit communication (often in tongues) and the Holy Spirit is helping us and interceding for us (Rom 8:22, 26). Jesus said,

And from the days of John the Baptist until now the kingdom of heaven has been treated violently, and violent men take it by force. Matt 11:12

Travail is the forceful and violent type of prayer that will not give up until there is breakthrough.

Dear God, is there something for which You are calling me to travail today?

Week 28, Day 2: Wrestling with God

Then Jacob was left alone, and a man wrestled with him until daybreak. When the man saw that he had not prevailed against him, he touched the socket of Jacob's hip; and the socket of Jacob's hip was dislocated while he wrestled with him. Then he said, 'Let me go, for the dawn is breaking.' But he said, "I will not let you go unless you bless me."
Genesis 32:24-26

God had given Jacob a mighty revelation of Himself and a promise of inheritance at Bethel on his outward journey (Gen 28:10-22). Now he was returning to Israel and contending to re-enter the land and claim his inheritance. Before he could do that, he had to face his brother and reconcile with the one he had hurt, who was also desperate for God's blessing.

Jacob had stolen his twin brother's birthright and his father's blessing, then spent twenty years living in exile with his relatives in Mesopotamia. He had been deceived by his uncle there but blessed by God and was now returning home. He was paranoid with fear when he heard his brother was coming to meet him. What sort of reception would he receive? Had Esau forgiven him or was he still wanting to kill him? Jacob humbled himself, prayed and wrestled with God alone all night. As he wrestled, Jacob prevailed but he was changed to the extent that God gave him a new name – Israel (Gen 32:28). Jacob had stolen a blessing, but now he wrestled to gain a blessing from God and his brother. In response to his prayer, God spoke to Esau and the two brothers were reconciled, albeit with Jacob emerging with a limp to remind him of the struggle and to keep him humble.

Travail is the struggle that causes us to be changed and allows God to work in the situation to bring the outcome for which we are praying. Are there obstacles standing between you and receiving your inheritance that need addressing, as with Jacob?

Father, show me what I need to contend for, and how that needs to be done.

Week 28, Day 3: Way of no return

And He [the LORD] said, 'My presence shall go with you, and I will give you rest.' Then he [Moses] said to Him, "If Your presence does not go with us, do not lead us up from here." Exodus 33:14-15

Once labour begins, you can't stop it until the birth. Travail also cannot give up until it sees a result. However, it must be a burden that the Lord has put on us and not one that we impose on ourselves that is not ours to carry. If not, it could break us, rather than us breaking through.

Moses contended for his people. After they made the golden calf and began to worship it, Moses went to the tent of meeting to intercede for them. God said He would not go with them on their journey because of their obstinance (Ex 33:3). However, God heard Moses' pleas and relented. His presence would accompany them on their journey (Ex 33:13-14). It is the presence of God that makes us different from all other people on the earth. Without that, we are indistinguishable from the world (Ex 33:16). If God does not go with us, we cannot go on. To do so would not only be unfruitful but foolish and dangerous as we would lose the cover of the Father's hand.

The Lord will challenge us to move forward in faith with Him, which will always be scary as it involves risk. If we do not move with God or we desire to return to our past land of Egypt, we are in trouble. The presence of God will leave, and we will lose our peace and our power. Backsliding is not an option. We must press on to the end goal with all our determination.

And Jesus said unto him, 'No man, having put his hand to the plough, and looking back, is fit for the kingdom of God.' Lk 9:62 (KJV)

Father, renew my love for You. Let it deepen daily and never become lukewarm. Rev 3:15-19

Week 28, Day 4: Birthing the promise

But Elijah went up to the top of Carmel; and he bent down to the earth and put his face between his knees. And he said to his servant, 'Go up now, look toward the sea.' So he went up and looked, but he said, "There is nothing." Yet Elijah said, 'Go back' seven times. And when he returned the seventh time, he said, "Behold, a cloud as small as a person's hand is coming up from the sea." 1 Kings 18:42b-44a

There had not been rain in the land for over three years and there was none on the horizon. God promised to send rain again but not before Elijah had confronted the king with his idolatry, challenged and shamed the *baals* in which they trusted, displayed God's authority in the fire of the sacrifice and killed the false prophets who promoted this idol worship. Elijah then predicted rain, but he had to engage in travail before it eventuated. He got down on his knees with his head between his knees and prayed seven times before his servant reported seeing the first cloud. He hung in there to birth the promise.

Often things do not happen as fast as we would like them to, and we wonder why. Sometimes natural births are relatively quick, and at other times the process is much longer than we want also. Elijah must have wondered why God did not answer the first time. But he had God's word, and he just kept praying. So must we.

Lord, is there something You have promised that I need to labour a bit more to see birthed?

Week 28, Day 5: Believing for the supernatural

...Even your relative Elizabeth herself has conceived a son in her old age, and she who was called infertile is now in her sixth month. For nothing will be impossible with God. Luke 1:36-37

Travail is often needed to birth the supernatural. Elizabeth was one of six women mentioned in the Bible who were barren. She birthed John the Baptist. All the three mothers of the patriarchs were barren – Sarah birthed Isaac in old age (Gen 21:1-2), at least 24 years after Abraham was promised a son. Rebekah gave birth to Jacob and Esau (Gen 25:21, 24-26a). Rachel produced Joseph and Benjamin after many years of infertility (Gen 30:24, 35:18). The sons of the covenant were birthed not by natural means but by supernatural. When God wants to do something supernatural, He does not use ordinary means to do it. If we want to experience miracles, we have to believe for the supernatural.

Two other biblical figures were also born to barren women. Manoah's wife birthed Samson (Judges 13:2-5) and Hannah's tears and vow to God led to Samuel's birth (1 Sam 1:5, 20).

If your life is barren, then ask God what supernatural things He wants to do to bring prosperity in its place. Prepare for Him to say something that seems impossible, and expect that you will need to travail to contend for it to come about. Nothing is impossible to God. Dispel the barrenness and call in the blessing.

Abba Father, help me to believe for the supernatural to break into my life and to contend for what You want to birth in and through me.

Week 28, Day 6: Agony

He withdrew about a stone's throw beyond them, knelt down and prayed, 'Father, if you are willing, take this cup from me; yet not my will, but yours be done.' An angel from heaven appeared to him and strengthened him. And being in anguish, he prayed more earnestly, and his sweat was like drops of blood falling to the ground. Luke 22:41-44 (NIV)

In the garden of Gethsemane Jesus was in the agony of travail as He battled in His soul to surrender to the excruciating pain of the cross, in order for God's purposes to be done and our freedom to be won. He suffered as a man and had to resist the temptation of taking the easy way out. In doing so, He understands our temptations (Heb 2:18). His obedience led to victory over Satan and death, and He now has the keys to Hades.

I am the first and the last, and the living One; and I was dead, and behold, I am alive forevermore, and I have the keys of death and of Hades. Rev 1:17c-18

In the process of travail, we die to ourselves, surrender to God's perfect will and birth His new life in us that overcomes the power of the enemy and releases resurrection creative power to change situations. We can never do what Jesus did for us but can join with Him in birthing the Kingdom of God in our lives, those of others and in our nation. We have been given keys to the Kingdom and we need to use them (Matt 16:19).

Thank You, Lord, for the agony You went through on my behalf. Make me willing to agonise if needed to birth your Kingdom on earth.

Week 28, Day 7: The breaking of the waters

Then David came to Baal-perazim and defeated them [the Philistines] there; and he said, 'The LORD has broken through my enemies before me like the breakthrough of waters.' Therefore, he named that place Baal-perazim. 2 Samuel 5:20

The birth is imminent when the waters break. Travail in prayer is not just any burden that we may labour under, it is always something which precedes birthing the Kingdom of God on earth. When David became king over all Israel, the Philistine enemies of Israel came *en masse* to contend against this godly king and his newly established kingdom.

We have an enemy who wants to destroy any effort to bring righteousness and godliness into our lives or our society. This is why we must resist the devil and fight for the things of the Kingdom of God. Revival and reformation will only come to our nation if we are willing to learn to travail and agonise in prayer and action, to be used of God to see our destiny fulfilled and that of our nation.

The darkest night occurs before the dawn. The hardest labour precedes the birth, but the joy of new life is the reward. When we see the waters break, the breakthrough is coming and cannot be stopped. Let there be a gush of many waters from heaven as His Kingdom begins to break forth on the earth.

And I heard a voice from heaven, like the sound of many waters and like the sound of loud thunder, and the voice which I heard was like the sound of harpists playing on their harps. Rev 14:2

Heavenly Father, teach me to contend for the birthing of your Kingdom on earth as it is in heaven.

Appendix

Prayer to commit your life to Jesus:

Dear God, I want to know you personally, not just have a head knowledge of you. I acknowledge that I have fallen short of your standards and I repent for my sin. I thank you that Jesus has died in my place to pay the price for my sin and set me free. I accept His sacrifice for me as my Saviour with thanksgiving. I realise that to come close to you, I must turn away from my selfish ways and I give you my heart to come and be Lord of my life. I thank you for sending your Holy Spirit to lead and guide me in this new life you are calling me into. In Jesus' name I pray. Amen

Prayer to be filled with the Holy Spirit:

Heavenly Father, I come to you asking that you would flood my life and fill me with your Holy Spirit. Work your cleansing in my life so the channels of living water can flow freely through me and produce the fruit of the Spirit in my life. I pray that you will give me also the gifts of the Spirit as you see fit for me and for those you want me to minister to in your name. I welcome the Holy Spirit into my life to have His way and move through me. I ask in Jesus' name, Amen

Table of Contents - Part 2

The *Many Facets of Prayer* continues with Part 2. This can be purchased from www.giftsfortheking.com.au or online from booksellers.

Workplace prayer

29. **Prayers of the Kingdom** The spread of the Kingdom; The gospel of the Kingdom; The nature of the Kingdom; The concept of the Kingdom; The ways of the Kingdom; Your Kingdom come on earth; Reigning with Christ

30. **The seven mountains of influence** Discipling nations; Worldview and culture; Religion; Family; The restoration of value; Education; Restoring morality

31. **Prayer in the workplace** The value of work; Business/Economy; Work to give; Arts and entertainment; One voice; Media; What is truth?

Spiritual Warfare

32. **Authority in Christ** Born to rule; Ecclesia, Seated with Him; All authority; Authority over evil powers; Knowing our boundaries; Uprooting and planting

33. **The weapons of our warfare** Our arsenal; The name of Jesus; The blood of Jesus; The word of God; Worship warfare; Mindsets; The opposite spirit

34. **The courts of heaven** The heavenly courtroom; Satan the accuser; Bringing down arguments; Two or three witnesses; Binding and loosing; Jesus' teaching on the courtroom; Defeating Satan

35. **Breakthrough prayer** Overcomers; Evidence of curses; Defiled land – Idolatry; Broken covenants; Innocent bloodshed; Immorality; Cleansing our bloodline

Praying for cities and regions

36. **Watchman prayer** Call of the watchman; Observing and listening; Warning; Watching over His Word; Recording and researching; Watching over Israel; Watching for the Bridegroom

37. **Prayer walking** The earth is the Lord's; Satan is a usurper; Reclaiming the land; Creation groans; Changing the spiritual atmosphere; Taking responsibility; Understanding the times

38. **Spiritual mapping** Spiritual mapping; Healing the land; The strategies of Satan; Powers and principalities; Breaking strongholds; Redeeming the land; Unlocking destiny

39. **Gatekeeping** Gates and gatekeepers; Courts of law; City gates; Gates of the temple; Guarding; Place of the prophets; Possessing the gates

40. **City-wide prayer** Transformation is possible; Inter-church prayer and worship; Breaking 'my church' mentality; Repentance; Unity – common purpose; Community concerns; Repairers and restorers

Prophetic Prayer

41. **Moving in the prophetic** That all would prophesy; Start small; Examine the spirits; The ministry of prophecy; The language of prophecy; Prophetic worship; Speaking forth destiny

42. **Proclaiming and declaring** Declaration and proclamation; The power of the enduring Word; Releasing faith; The prophetic role in prayer; Praying prophecies into being; Oceania; Declarations over nations

43. **Praying through dreams and visions** Symbols; Warning dreams; Parables; Last days' outpouring; Refining character; God reveals secrets; Visions of heaven

44. **Prophetic intercession** Priest and prophet; God's appointed times; Contending for His return; Contending for the harvest; Contending for the bride; Contending for Israel; Contending for Australia

45. **Prophetic assignments** The purpose of prophetic assignments; Signs of the covenant; Holding up a mirror; Prophetic of things to come; Examples of assignments; Blood covering; Sealing

Praying for nations

46. **Identificational repentance** National sins; Ezra; Nehemiah; Daniel; Identifying as part of a group; Historical repentance; National days of repentance

47. **The war cabinet** Warrior God; Army training; Territorial strongholds; Know your enemy; Deception; Binding the strongman; Re-digging the wells

48. **Praying for government** All authority; The purpose of government; Righteousness and justice; How to pray; Our responsibility; Legislate in the Spirit; The government of God

49. **Praying for Israel** God's eternal covenant; God's chosen people; Israel's physical return; Israel's spiritual return; Grafted in; Key to world revival; Welcoming the Messiah

50. **Praying for nations** All nations; The return of the Lord; Sheep and goat nations; The ends of the earth; Australia's Christian foundations; Prophetic words; Breaking curses over the nation

51. **The apostolic role in prayer** Decrees; Overthrowing and building; For such a time as this; Cyrus and Darius; Authority of God's prophetic word; Apostolic authority; Writing a decree

52. **Establishing a house of prayer** A dwelling place for the Lord; Birthing a house of prayer; A tabernacle of David; A house of prayer for all people; Building a team; Pray without ceasing; Come Lord Jesus

Endnotes

Week 1
- Day 1 1. Prayer to commit your life to Jesus as your Saviour and Lord – See Appendix Page 228
- Day 3 2. Prayer to be filled with the Holy Spirit – See Appendix Page 228

Week 4
- Day 3 1. www.i4give.com
- Day 7 2. www.statista.com/statistics/1417207/australia-frequency-of-pornography-use-over-the-past-year-by-young-people

Week 9
- Day 5 1. www.ctntp.uk/wp-content/uploads/2017/12/seven-national-calls-to-prayer-in-wwii.pdf
  www.presidency.ucsb.edu/documents/proclamation-97-appointing-day-national-humiliation-fasting-and-prayer

Week 10
- Day 1 1. Webb, R., *Grumble Fast*, Heart of the Psalmist Inc, Vic, 2020
- Day 2 2. Voskamp, A., *One Thousand Gifts*, Zondervan, Michigan, 2010

Week 12
1. William Temple, *Nature, Man and God*. www.goodreads.com/quotes/441116-to-worship-is-to-quicken-the-conscience-by-the-holiness

Week 16
- Day 3 1. www.azquotes.com/author/20531-Alexander_Fraser_Tytler
- Day 4 2. Grubb, N., *Rees Howells, Intercessor*, Lutterworth Press, Cambridge UK, 1952

Week 18
- Day 4 1. www.beersheba100.com.au/anzacs/anzac-values.html
- Day 7 2. www.worldwithoutgenocide.org/genocides-and-conflicts/the-ottoman-christian-genocide

Week 20
- Day 4 1. www.abs.gov.au/statistics/people/people-and-communities/household-and-families-census/latest-release
  2. www.abs.gov.au/statistics/people/crime-and-justice/partner-violence/latest-release
- Day 7 3. www.opendoors.org/en-US/persecution/countries

4. www.barnabasaid.org/au
5. www.opendoors.org.au/?gad_source=1&gclid=EAIaIQobChMI9rP6v-WmiwMVaaRmAh0LiBr2EAAYASAAEgJlUfD_BwE
6. www.azquotes.com/author/20566-Martin_Niemoller

Week 22
    Day 1 1. Grubb, N., *Rees Howells, Intercessor*, Lutterworth Press Cambridge UK, 1952, P 86

Week 24
    Day 6 1. Chapman, G., *The Five Languages of Love*, Northfield Press, Mass, 1992

Week 25
    Day 7 1. www.partnersinprayer.org.au/revive-melbourne-again-lord

Week 26
    Day 1 1. Klein, J., & Spears, A., *Lost in Translation Vol 1, Rediscovering the Hebrew Roots of our Faith*, Covenant Research Institute, OR, 2007, chapter 4

Bibliography

Benge, J&G., *Count Zinzendorf*, YWAM Pub, Seattle, WA, 2005

Blackaby, H&R., *Hearing God's Voice*, Broadman & Holman Pub, Nashville, 2002

Blackaby, H&R., *Experiencing God*, Broadman & Holman Pub, Nashville, 2008

Bridges, J., *Respectable Sins*, NavPress, CO, 2007

Cahn, J., *The Return of the gods*, Frontline, Florida, 2022

Chadwick, B., (ed), *Torrey on Prayer*, Bridge Logos, Florida, 2009

Chapman, G., *The Five Languages of Love*, Northfield Press, Mass, 1992

Connor, K.J., *The Foundations of Christian Doctrine*, Acacia Press, Blackburn, Vic, 1980

Curry, J., *All Israel shall be Saved*, J Curry, Melbourne, 2020

Curry, J., (Ed) *Keys to Australia's Destiny*, J Curry, Melbourne, 2022

Curry, J., *The Anzac Call*, J Curry, Melbourne, 2016

Dawson, J., *Taking our Cities for God*, Creation House, Florida, 1989

Enlow, J., *The Seven Mountain Prophecy*, Creation House, Florida, 2008

Frangipane, F., *The Three battlegrounds*, Advancing Church Pub, USA

Frankovic, J., *The Kingdom of Heaven*, Jerusalem Bible Class Series, HaKesher Inc, OK, 1998

Grubb, N., *Rees Howells, Intercessor*, Lutterworth Press, Cambridge UK, 1952

Henderson, R., *Impacting the Seven Mountains from the Courts of Heaven*, Destiny Image, 2023

Henderson, R., *Operating in the Courts of Heaven*, Robert Henderson Min, USA, 2014

Henderson, R., *Unlocking Destinies from the Courts of Heaven*, Robert Henderson Min, USA, 2016

Hess, T., *The Watchmen*, Morning Star Pub., NC, 1998

Hubbard, J. Dr., *Moravian Miracle*, Australian Heart Pub., NSW, 2022

Jacobs, C., *The Reformation Manifesto*, Bethany House Pub, Minnesota, 2008

Klein, J., & Spears, A., *Lost in Translation Vol 1, Rediscovering the Hebrew Roots of our Faith*, Covenant Research Institute, OR, 2007

Ladd, G.E., *The Gospel of the Kingdom*, Paternoster Press, London, 1959

Lewis, C.S., *The Screwtape Letters*, Collins, Glasgow, 1942

Liardon, R., *The Smith Wigglesworth Prophecy & the Greatest Revival of all Time*, Whitaker House, PA, 2013

Mangalwadi, V., *The Book that made your World*, Thomas Nelson, Tennessee, 2011

Mangalwadi, V., *Truth and Transformation*, YWAM Pub, Seattle, 2009

Meyer, J., *Battlefield of the Mind*, Faith Words, New York, 1995

Miller, B., *Decrees and Dangerous Prayers*, Barbara Miller Books, QLD, 2022   www.barbara-miller-books.com/product/decrees-and-dangerous-prayers

Miller, B., *The European Quest to find Terra Australia Incognita*, Writersandebooks, Sydney, 2014

Murray, A., *The Prayer Life*, Moody Press, Chicago, (no date given)

Newbold, C. Jr, *The Crucified Ones*, Ingathering Press, Tennessee, 1990

Otis, G Jr., *Informed Intercession*, Renew, California, 1999

Packer, J.I., *Knowing God*, Hodder and Stoughton, London, 1973

Prince, D., *Shaping History through Prayer and Fasting*, Whitaker House, NC, 1973

Prince, D., *The Power of Proclamation*, Derek Prince Min, NSW, 2002

Prince, D., *The Last Word on the Middle East*, Kingsway Pub, 1982

Ridings, R&P., *Shifting Nations through Houses of Prayer*, CHI books, QLD, 2019

Sheets, D., *Authority in Prayer*, Bethany House, Minnesota, 2006

Stone, P., *Angels on Assignment*, Charisma House, Florida, 1982

Stringer, C., *Smith Wigglesworth in Australia and New Zealand*, Col Stringer Min, QLD, 2009

Thompson, A.F., & Beale, A., *The Divinity Code*, Destiny Image Pub, PA, 2011

Tozer, A.W., *The Knowledge of the Holy*, Kingsway Pub, Eastbourne, UK, 1961

Tozer, A.W., *The Pursuit of God*, OM Pub, 1982

Voskamp, A., *One Thousand Gifts*, Zondervan, Michigan, 2010

Wagner, C.P., *Prayer Shield*, Monarch, California, 1992

Wagner, C.P. (ed), *Breaking Strongholds in your City*, Regal Books, California, 1993

Wallis, A., *God's Chosen Fast*, Kingsway Pub, Eastbourne UK, 1989

Webb, R., *Grumble Fast*, Heart of the Psalmist Inc, Vic, 2020

Yun, Br., with Paul Hattaway, *The Heavenly Man*, Monarch Books, Michigan, 2002

Acknowledgements

My primary thanks goes to Jesus who has made it possible for us to enter the Holy of holies to have fellowship with the Father in heaven, the Creator of all things. Prayer is now our privilege as we can approach the throne room and enjoy intimate communication with God Almighty.

Bret Ridley is one of those rare gems who is willing to come alongside with amazing grace and patience to give his computer expertise to format and prepare the book for printing. Without his partnership, this book would just be words on my computer.

Susan Pierotti has also stood by me for many years to voluntarily contribute her professional editing skills to make sure the text is in order before printing. Thanks also to Gerredina Kovac, who has kindly and efficiently proofread all my books, Mirelle Curtis and Dianne Taylor for their initial proofreading.

Jenny Hagger has yet again been a tremendous encouragement and support for this project. She insists on making the time, not just for a cursory look or summary of the text but on reading every word before writing her endorsement. She is a true apostle of prayer and a gift to Australia and beyond. I also thank all the others who have taken the time to write endorsements – Warwick Marsh, Kym Farnik, Ken Duncan, Karen Wilson, Ruth Webb, and Barbara Miller and Hilary Moroney.

My local photo club president, Denise Perentin, is not only an amazing photographer but also a photoshop master and has generously helped to bring my vision into reality for the book cover.

I could not finish without thanking those who have prayed for this book as it has progressed from start to completion. I have experienced some serious battles along the way and trust that the end product will be a blessing to many and help raise up an army of prayer warriors who will answer God's call to intercede for His Kingdom to come on earth and our nations to fulfil their destiny.

About the author

Jill Curry is a teacher, author and prayer leader who has had the privilege of learning under some top global prayer leaders during her time living in Israel. She founded Shnat Ratzon Ministries (Year of the Lord's Favour) in 1998 as an Israel Intercessory Support Ministry. From 1997-2001 she lived in Israel, teaching at the 'School of Worship' in Jerusalem, and researching and writing *Prepare the Way for the King of Glory* with Tom Hess. She is the founder and coordinator of the *Jewish & Israel Prayer Focus* ministry which was birthed in 2002 from Australia. She has a  Masters in Higher Education, a Bachelor of Music and a Diploma of Ministry.

Jill has also written, *The Anzac Call* which outlines the significant part the ANZACs (Australian and New Zealand Army Corps) played in the Middle East in WW1, and connects this to the end-time prophecies of the Bible. It also calls for the raising up of the spiritual Anzac Army, and calls the church and nation to stand with Israel today. This is now out of print but the information and many resources can be found at www.beersheba100.com.au. She has also written *Designed Destiny* and *All Israel shall be Saved* and edited *Keys to Australia's Destiny*. Information for these is on the following page.

Other Materials by the Same Author

Available from www.giftsfortheking.com.au Click Books

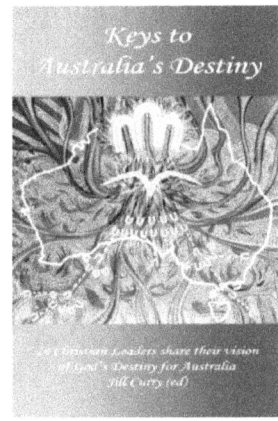

Keys to Australia's Destiny brings together twenty-four Australian leaders – apostles, prophets, pastors, evangelists, teachers and prayer leaders, indigenous and non-indigenous, mature and emerging, who share their vision of what they believe is God's destiny for Australia, New Zealand and the Pacific region and how we can fulfil His plan for our nations and region. Contributors include: Tim Edwards – indigenous leader, Jenny Hagger – apostle of prayer, Lana Vawser – Australia's most globally recognised prophet, Warwick Marsh – prayer leader and advocate for faith, family, freedom, and life, Bill Muehlenberg – culture commentator, Margaret Court – champion of tennis and faith who has stood unwaveringly for truth.

All Israel Shall be Saved explains God's purposes for the nation of Israel and provides monthly prayer topics and prayer points to pray for the redemption of Israel with articles by pastors and prayer leaders living in the land. You will see how prophecy is being fulfilled as God is working in the lives of Jews and Arabs to bring His Kingdom purposes to pass.

Understanding what destiny is, finding your place in this plan, and knowing how to practically walk it out are some of the most crucial decisions you will ever make in this life. *Designed Destiny* aims to help the young and the not-so-young who are searching for life's answers and want to embark on this exciting journey.

Also see www.beersheba100.com.au for information from *The Anzac Call* (now out of print)

www.ingramcontent.com/pod-product-compliance
Lightning Source LLC
Chambersburg PA
CBHW052019070526
44584CB00016B/1816